Motorbooks International
WARBIRD HISTORY

P-51 MUSTANG

Robert F. Dorr

First published in 1995 by Motorbooks International
Publishers & Wholesalers, PO Box 2, 729 Prospect Avenue,
Osceola, WI 54020 USA

Library of Congress Cataloging-in-Publication Data

Dorr, Robert F.
    P-51 Mustang/Robert F. Dorr.
        p. cm.
    Includes bibliographical references and index.
    ISBN 0-7603-0002-X (Pbk.)
    1. Mustang (Fighter planes) I. Title. II. Title: P-fifty-one
Mustang.
UG1242.F5D62   1995
623.7'464'0973—dc20   95-6118

On the front cover: F-51D Mustang 44-63674 flies over
Mount Fuji near Tokyo during the Korean era. *via Robert
Esposito*

On the title page: Surrounded by picturesque mountains,
F-51D Mustangs bask in the sun awaiting their missions at
Chinhae, Korea.

On the frontispiece: A camouflaged, red-nosed NAA P-
51D Mustang warming up. This aircraft carries two 500lb
(227kg) bombs and six 2.75in rocket tubes. The location
appears to be the NAA plant at Inglewood, California.
Rockwell

On the back cover, top: A natural-metal P-51D Mustang
carrying 2.75in, bazooka-style rocket tubes shows its
vulnerable underside to the camera on an apparent
proving flight from the manufacturer's Inglewood,
California, facility. This view, from an angle rarely seen,
shows under-wing pylons, discard openings for the six
.50cal (12.7mm) wing machine guns, and the coolant
radiator housing that makes the Mustang so susceptible to
ground-based antiaircraft fire. *Rockwell*

On the back cover, bottom: In his painting *Tuskegee Red-
Tailed Devil*, artist recalls a 332nd FG mission by a P-51D
Mustang that is escorting B-24 Liberators and is flown by
Capt. Lewis R. Purnell. The Negro Americans of the 332nd
established a superb combat record and demonstrated in
both air-to-air and air-to-ground missions that the
Mustang was one of the finest fighters of World War II.
These courageous pilots also paved the way for an end to
a segregated military service, which happened soon after
the war. Copies of *Tuskegee Red Tail Angel* are available
from Windswept Wings, 7020 Hames Court, Frederick,
Maryland 21701. *David Sample*

Printed in Hong Kong

Contents

Acknowledgments

This book is an attempt at a general history of the design, development, and operational and combat use of the North American P-51 Mustang.

Because this is history, every attempt is made to use terms and expressions for the period covered. Military ranks, assignments, and nomenclature are given for the time covered.

Thousands of facts appear on these pages. Any errors are the sole responsibility of this author. But the book would have been impossible without help.

Among the fraternity: Gerry F. Beels, Warren M. Bodie, Alan Bovelt, William Brafford, Jr., Bill Crimmins, Brian Cull, Larry Davis, Robert Esposito, Jeffrey L. Ethell, Robert B. Greby, Norm Green, Dan Hagedorn, Robert Hewson, John Hunt, Ken Hutchison, Kyle Kirby, Jon Lake, Robert L. Lawson, Harold G. Martin, Ken A. McLean, David W. Menard, Joseph E. Michaels, Robert C. Mikesh, R. J. Mills, Lars Olausson, Merle C. Olmsted, Steve Pace, Terry Panopalis, Robert J. Pickett, Bruce Potts, Jim Sullivan, Arnold Swanberg, Norman Taylor, Nick Veronico, and L. J. Vosloo.

The following were interviewed: Devol Brett (39th FBS/18th FBW); Vern Brown (41st FS/35th FG); Michael P. Curphey (375th FS/361st FG); Joseph H. Fahey (78th FS/15th FG); Thomas Hayes (364th FS/357th FG); Bill Holloman (99th FS/332nd FG); Brad Hood (Vintage Fighters); Jack Ilfrey (79th FS/20th FG); Richard C. M. Lewer (No 2 Squadron, SAAF); Josh Reynolds (No. 122 Squadron, RAF); Frank Speer (4th FG); Stanley Vashina; and Leonard A. Wood (375th FS/361st FG).

The following shared their experiences via correspondence or by telephone: Randy Acord (Cold Weather Test Detachment); Jim Beasley (civil Mustang); Duane E. (Bud) Biteman (25th FS/51st FG); Don Botsford (363rd TRW); Robert C. Brown (67th FBS/18th FBW); Ron Brown (3-7th FS/31st FG); McCauley Clark (38th FS/55th FG); Dan Leftwich (384th FS/364th FG); Ron Purssey (No. 23 Squadron, RAAF); Ralph H. Saltsman, Jr., (18th FBG); and William Spencer (334th FS/4th FG).

Special thanks are due Rockwell International's Erik Simonsen and Chris Wamsley, who went overboard to help with this effort. Also to Maj. Elizabeth Lourens of *Nyala*, the SAAF's flying safety magazine and Ross Macpherson of *New Zealand Wings* magazine for permission to adapt material. Also, to Col. Peter J. (Monster) Wilkins of the SAAF, Tim Parker, and Michael Dregni.

The author is indebted to artist Heinz Krebs, for permission to use his color painting *Checkmate*, copies of which are available from Art-Haus, 6541 North Cibola Avenue, Tucson, Arizona 85718, telephone (602) 529-1432.

The author is also indebted to artist David Sample, for permission to use his color painting *Tuskegee Red-Tailed Angel*, copies of which can be obtained from Windswept Wings, 7020 Hames Court, Frederick, Maryland 21701.

Perhaps the greatest debt of all is to Brad C. Hood, who flew this author on two sorties in Charles Osborn's P-51D Mustang *Hurry Home, Honey*. These flights in a P-51 were made possible by the annual "Warbirds Over Hickory" air show, sponsored by the Sabre Society of North Carolina, a fine group of ardent enthusiasts and historians who put on our country's best "warbird" show and are also working to restore aircraft and create a museum. Anyone who'd like to learn about this nonprofit undertaking should contact the Sabre Society of North Carolina, P. O. Box 1968, Hickory, North Carolina 28603.

The views expressed in this book are mine and do not necessarily reflect those of the United States Air Force.

Robert F. Dorr
Oakton, Virginia

CHAPTER 1

Design and Development of the P-51 Mustang

In 1939, Britain needed fighters. The Second World War was spreading, even while many Americans sought to ignore it or to stay out of it.

Sir Henry Self of British Purchasing Commission was posted to New York to see how American industry could help his country's war needs. Barely had he arrived when Self began seeing terms like "urgent" and "high priority" in dispatches reaching him from home.

The team of British purchasers found only two American fighters that might be of some use to the Royal Air Force (RAF). Neither was ideal. The Bell P-39 Airacobra and Curtiss P-40 Warhawk were not up to the standards of performance of the latest British and German fighters, but they were the best that America had to offer.

The British and French governments placed orders in 1940 for 1,740 Curtiss P-36 Hawk pursuit ships, but neither country was satisfied with the performance of these aircraft. The British also purchased small numbers of Airacobras. In April 1940, Self, wanting more and better planes, concluded the manufacturers he'd talked to, so far, had no more production capacity to offer him.

Among Self's contacts was manufacturer North American Aviation (NAA) in Inglewood, California, which was doing a superb job of building trainers but had no track record in the design and construction of warplanes.

Self's 1939 discussions with the manufacturing firm's president and general manager, James H. (Dutch) Kindelberger, marked the start of events that led to the design of the NAA P-51 Mustang. The British visited NAA to ask if Kindelberger's firm could open up a new production line for P-40s. They were told it would take 120 days to tool up for this purpose.

Dutch Kindelberger had visited the Heinkel and Messerschmitt aircraft factories in 1938 and had taken notes on how the Germans were developing fighters with liquid-cooled engines. Kindelberger convinced the British that instead of gearing up to build P-40s, North America should embark on a more dramatic course. Given 120 days, Kindelberger said—with no evidence to prove his point, for it had never been done before—a completely new and better fighter could be built specifically to British needs. It would have higher speed and rate of climb, improved maneuverability up to higher speeds, and increased range and firepower.

The British approved a preliminary design by NAA on 4 May 1940. They followed up with a contract for 320 of these pursuit ships, built against NAA contract NA-73, on 29 May 1940.

For nearly half a century afterward, accolades bestowed upon the spirited filly from Ingelwood told us the Mustang was a "120-day wonder," dreamed up, designed, rolled out, and test-flown within the incredibly brief span of four months. A few detailed histories, often only in fine print, told us that this high-speed miracle occurred, in part, because Sir Henry Self secured cooperation from a more experienced maker of pursuit ships, the Curtiss firm in Buffalo.

There is dispute over just what it meant, but there is not argument that NAA's design team had access to Curtiss documents on the P-40, which had been Britain's original choice. The original P-40, designed by Curtiss' Don Berlin, had had its liquid cooling radiator below the fuselage, just under the pilot—a configuration rejected by US Army Air Corps (USAAC) as rendering the pursuit ship too vulnerable to ground fire. The decision cannot be faulted. No one knew in the late 1930s that the mission that would become more important than all others was high-altitude escort to Berlin. Having a radiator right under the center of the aircraft was, beyond question, a high-risk proposition, as Mustang pilots in Korea were to learn a short decade later.

An operational P-51D Mustang prepares to taxi out. *Rockwell*

But the British were not bound by a USAAC decision. This became the configuration of the new NAA airplane—and its principal weakness throughout production of 15,463 airplanes.

Rapid Design

The legend persists that NAA vice president J. Leland Atwood and a masterful design team (led by Edgar Schmued and Raymond Rice) cooked up the Mustang from scratch and created it at lightning speed. In fact, Atwood spent months working with the British and with the Curtiss firm. Curtiss designer Don Berlin had created another sleek fighter called the XP-46, and Atwood gained access to it. Because it would have been uneconomical to halt P-40 production to introduce the only marginally better-performing XP-46, wind tunnel data on Berlin's fighter were sold to NAA in April 1940 for $56,000.

It requires no graduate diploma in engineering to see that the XP-46 and P-51 look very much alike, but the sale of data and the full magnitude of the Curtiss/Don Berlin contribution to the Mustang remain in dispute even today.

Atwood and Kindelberger presented the British with a preliminary design less than four months after the blueprints were approved by the British Purchasing Commission. Contrary to myth, no plan existed to complete the prototype Mustang in 120 days. This should not detract from the fact that the first aircraft was completed very rapidly and was, in almost every respect, a superb fighter design.

Some 78,000 engineering hours and 127 days went into the first ship, which was rolled into the sunlight at Mines Field in Los Angeles on 9 September 1940. So hastily had the new fighter been assembled, it had no engine (until a couple of weeks later) and rolled on wheels borrowed from an AT-6 trainer. This first ship was known to its maker as the NA-73X and wore civil registry number NX19998. Powered by an Allison V-1710-F3R engine, the prototype made its first flight on 26 October 1940 at Mines Field in Los Angeles, with Vance Breese as pilot.

AG633 was the 290th Mustang built, counting the NA-73X prototype, and retained the early configuration of Allison-powered fighters. Cruising over a quiltwork of English countryside wearing the code XV-E, this sleek Mustang I was assigned to No. 2 Squadron, RAF ACC. The white spinner, yellow leading edges, and British tail flash are all typical of the era. Two aircraft from this same batch evolved into the first USAAF Mustangs, and were designated XP-51. British doctrine never called for the long range offered by the Mustang, so the shorter-range Spitfire continued to enjoy priority in the RAF's purchasing plans. *RAF Museum*

With Vance Breese grasping the stick, the NA-73X prowls a California coast devoid of smog or freeways. This portrait was taken between the Mustang's inaugural flight on 26 October 1940 and its crack-up, caused by fuel starvation, on 20 November 1940 amid flight number nine. The NA-73X was rebuilt, still in natural metal with no distinctive insignia, and resumed test flying on 11 January 1941. A document from the era indicates that NAA put a "base airplane" price of $37,590 on the fighters it was selling the British. *Rockwell*

By this time, France had fallen beneath the German onslaught. The need for better-performing fighters was critical.

But there seemed little about the all-silver NA-73X to mark it as a quantum leap forward. A low-wing, flush-canopy, liquid-cooled ship, the NA-73X introduced no real design innovations and looked more or less the same as any other fighter in its class, Spitfire and Messerschmitt Bf 109 included. The NA-73X did offer great promise, mostly because its designers borrowed good ideas and used them well. Among these was a low, square-cut wing whose laminar-flow airfoil reduced drag and a radiator scoop streamlined into the lower fuselage behind the pilot.

Though the progenitor of this fighter series had been designed for a greater fuel load than many of its contemporaries, the extra weight proved to be no impediment. Test pilot Breese was delighted when the NA-73X attained a speed of 382mph (614 km/h), making it as fast as early Spitfires that carried half as much fuel.

The life of NX19998 was to be cut short, however. On flight number nine, 20 November 1940, pilot Paul Balfour made an error in switching fuel-feed, and the engine went dead at a critical moment. Balfour had no time to attempt a re-start before aircraft and ground came together. The NA-73X piled up in an upside-down wreck. Unhurt, Balfour was more annoyed than worried as he clambered out of the inverted fighter. A major delay had just been introduced into the Mustang development program, although the NA-73X did, in fact, resume flying on 11 January 1941 and continued to operate as part of the initial development program until being retired on 15 July 1941.

The NA-73 was ordered into production for the RAF on 20 September 1940 under terms that specified that two examples would be delivered for testing to the US Army, designated XP-51. The first of these (41-038, also assigned British serial AG348) flew on 20 May 1941 at Inglewood piloted by Robert Chilton.

The NA-73X is pushed through the sky over Los Angeles by test pilot Vance Breese. The NA-73X completed a total of 45 flights before being retired on 15 July 1941. Experimental flying was taken over beginning in April 1941 by the first British Mustang I, serial AG345. This meant that the second production ship, AG346, was the first to be shipped to Britain. The NA-73X had a single-piece windshield structure (although this view could give the mistaken impression of a horizontal bar near its top) while subsequent Mustangs had canopy bracing up front and a flat windshield plate. *Rockwell*

An early, Allison-powered Mustang in flight in USAAF camouflage with the early national insignia used prior to addition of a bar to the roundel in 1943. *USAF*

Careful scrutiny of this sleek RAF pursuit ship reveals four 20mm cannons jutting forward in a very prominent way from the leading edge, rather than the six .50cal (12.7mm) machine-guns that were standard armament on most British and American Mustangs. On the heels of its initial "buy" of Mustangs I models, Britain ordered 150 Mustangs against NAA's NA-91 contract. In July 1942, the first deliveries began of this Mustang IA model. This aesthetic Mustang IA has yet to receive individual squadron codes. *RAF Museum*

P-51 Program

Early plans for the new NAA fighter called for delivery of 620 production machines, given the name Mustang Mk I by the British. Power was provided by a 1,150hp Allison V-1710-39 liquid-cooled engine driving a three-blade propeller. A roll-out took place on 16 April 1941. First flight of a Mustang I for the RAF (AG345), retaining the company designation NA-73, was made on 23 April 1941 at Inglewood by Louis Wait. The first ship to be delivered (AG346) reached Liverpool on 24 October 1941.

This first Mustang to reach England was a test ship for many to follow. Assembled at RAF Burton-wood, AG346 received a British radio and other minor changes in internal equipment. Though service ceiling at this time was limited to 30,000ft (9,288m), British pilots were pleased with the fighter, noting only that camouflage paint slowed its maximum air-

speed by some 8mph (13km/h). Initial test results showed that the American fighter could reach a speed of 375mph (604km/h) at 15,000ft (4,644m) as compared to the British Spitfire Mk V, which topped out at 240mph (548km/h) at the same height.

Looking back, it's debatable whether Britain needed so many Mustangs so early when the Spitfire was on its way to becoming more numerous (over 20,000 built) than any American fighter of the war. When Sir Henry Self's purchasing team contracted for the Mustang, the Battle of Britain was not yet joined, its outcome by no means assured. "Worst case" thinking had to include Germany taking over the United Kingdom, including its production facilities, with the RAF exiled to foreign shores to press on with the fight. A more optimistic view might have looked ahead to the Allies turning the tide and invading occupied Europe. Either way, the Spitfire never had the range or load-carrying capability of the Mustang and was never ideal for long-distance missions.

On the minus side of the ledger, the Spitfire could climb to 20,000ft (6,192m) in 7min, while the Mustang required 11min. Both the Spitfire and Messerschmitt Bf 109 were deemed more nimble at higher altitude. The Mustang, which weighed about a third again as much as a Spitfire, was considered to be underpowered.

Close-up details of early Mustangs: the cockpit of the Allison-powered P-51A Mustang [**above left**] looks quite comfortable but offers even less visibility than one might expect. Note the modified vent window in the left front windshield and the absence of radio gear behind the armored seat back. The canopy of the Merlin-powered P-51B Mustang [**above right**] is typical of the "bird-cage" configu- ration found on all early aircraft. Details of the landing gear and lower front of a P-51A model [**below**] include three-blade propeller, wing gun ports, main undercarriage, and nose shape. From the very beginning, the Mustang exuded a sleek, aerodynamic appearance. *Rockwell*

The 321st NAA Mustang I (AL958) for Britain's RAF, attired in USAAF insignia, flies over California mountains in late 1942 or early 1943. Allison-powered Mustangs all had a distinctive, elongated air scoop above the propeller hub. All flush-canopy Mustangs were built without the dorsal fillet found on the bubble-canopy P-51D that were built later. This ship was widely featured in publicity photos but was not one of the two Mustang Is (AG348, AG354) delivered to the USAAF under the designation XP-51. *Rockwell*

When it approved the Mustang I for British use, the US Army specified that two planes were to be put into American hands, at no cost, for flight evaluation. Before this could take place, Britain ordered an additional 150 Mustangs against the manufacturer's NA-91 contract. In these aircraft, machine gun armament was replaced with four wing-mounted 20mm cannon. In July 1942, the first deliveries began of this Mustang IA model.

The fourth and tenth airplanes from the NAA production run, now designated XP-51s, went to Wright Field, Ohio for tests. The US Army Air Forces, (USAAF) also ordered 500 dive-bomber versions of the new fighter, which they designated A-36 Apache. These were Mustangs powered by the 1,325hp Allison V-1710-87 engine and fitted with large dive brakes on the wings. The USAAF also eventually received 57 of the airplanes from Britain's Mustang IA contract, of which 55 were modified with two F24 oblique cameras in the rear fuselage as F-6A Invader photo-reconnaissance aircraft.

Production of the A-36 Apache was undertaken in part to keep the Inglewood production line warm. Together with Kindelberger and Schmued, designer Stanley Worth had a strong hand in transforming North America's sleek pursuit ship into an American equivalent of the Stuka. The Mustang design had evolved with anything but the dive-bombing role in mind, yet the airframe lent itself well to installation of dive brakes and bomb shackles for two 500lb (228kg) bombs fitted under each wing beneath the trays for six .50cal (12.7mm) machine-guns. The A-36 Apache's dive brakes were of the lattice type, which opened both above and below the main wing giving well-stabilized control during a dive. Despite early hydraulic problems, the A-36 became a splendid dive-bomber and saw much combat in the Mediterranean and Far East in 1943–44.

P-51A Model

The P-51A designation went to the first ship in the US Army's stable to be built in at least modest numbers. Power came from a 1,200hp Allison V-1710-81 with an improved supercharger and introducing a larger Curtiss 10ft 9in (3.32m) three-blade propeller.

A NAA A-36A Apache dive bomber (42-83861) being pulled through the sky by an Allison V-1710-87 engine that was regarded as having more than adequate horsepower at low altitude. Not much of an answer to Germany's famous Junkers Ju 87 Stuka, the A-36 was put into production partly to keep the Mustang line going.

A-36 Apaches flew 23,373 combat sorties and dropped 8,000 tons of bombs in air campaigning over the Mediterranean and Southeast Asia. A respectably low total of 177 A-36s were lost to enemy air and ground action during World War II. *Rockwell*

The dynamic duo: not often posed in a side-by-side comparison on the ground are Merlin- (at left) and Allison-powered Mustangs. The P-51B at left sports a cleaned-up nose shape and four-blade propeller while the Mustang IA, or NA-91, at right has the scoop associated with Allison power, a three-blade prop, and somewhat different fuselage shape. This portrait was apparently snapped in the boondocks at Mines Field, which has since evolved into Los Angeles International Airport. *Rockwell*

P-51B Mustang in olive drab with light fuselage underside and the US national insignia that was used from 14 August 1943 until after the end of World War II. This view emphasizes the retractable main gear and tail wheel and the under-fuselage coolant area that kept the Mustang vulnerable to low-level ground fire throughout its combat career. *Rockwell*

This olive-drab NAA P-51B Mustang (43-12342) is having its Merlin engine run up on the parking ramp at Mines Field apparently in mid-1943. The national emblem with bar and shield insignia with red "surround" was authorized on American military aircraft only for a brief period (28 June 1943 to 14 August 1943), after which the "surround" was changed to insignia-blue, leaving US warplanes with no red at all to be confused in combat with the red of Japan's *hinomaru*, or "meatball." *Rockwell*

A striking top view of the flush-canopy, Merlin-powered P-51B Mustang carrying drop tanks on a flight over the Sierra Madre. The plan view of the Mustang changed little as new versions reached fighting forces. The clean wing design and more than adequate wing area helped to make the Mustang highly maneuverable at medium altitudes and, in most respects, the equal of the Messerschmitt Bf 109, even at higher altitudes where the German fighter performed best. *Rockwell*

Four .50cal (12.7mm) machine-guns were installed in the wings, with none in the nose. New 150gal drop tanks, coupled with the greater efficiency of the -81 version of the engine, raised the ferry range of the aircraft to 2,700mi (4,345km), giving pilots and planners their first taste of the long range that was to bring the Mustang, in time, to Berlin. The first P-51A, 43-6003, went aloft for the first time on 3 February 1942, piloted by Robert Chilton.

A batch of 310 of these P-51As (43-6003/6312) was ordered. Fifty were delivered to the RAF. These were designated Mustang Mk II (company NA-83) and the first British example (AL958) made its first flight at Inglewood on 13 February 1942 with Chilton

doing the honors. The early hydraulic difficulties were by now past history and the P-51A, in both American and British livery, performed well.

The A model or Mustang II was the final version of the fighter equipped with the Allison engine. In all, 1,570 Allison-powered Mustangs came from the builder, of which 764 went to Britain.

Long after other Mustangs were operational, a P-51A was the first of several models to be tested in Alaska by the Cold Weather Detachment, part of Materiel Command at Wright Field—with skis replacing conventional landing wheels for operations from ice surfaces. "The ski test was successful," remembers pilot Randy Acord, "but the advantages were limited. The ski loading was so high, the aircraft would not ride up on the snow. In soft, deep snow, propeller clearance was a problem.

"One interesting point," remembers Acord. "When skis slide on the snow, heat is produced and upon stopping the warm skis immediately froze to the snow-covered ground. To taxi again, it would require about 75 percent throttle to break loose the frozen skis. The small rudder would not hold the

This olive-drab P-51B Mustang (43-12102) was yanked off the production line and employed as the test ship for the bubble canopy P-51D model. Visibility was far from ideal in earlier versions and the absence of canopy stripping around the pilot gave him a far better view in all directions. *via M. J. Kasiuba*

torque and before the throttle could be reduced the torque would turn the aircraft approximately 45deg to the right of the path desired when taxiing again."

There was nothing wrong with the Allison engine, but the decision to switch to the superb British Merlin was a choice that illustrated the Mustang's growth potential. In April 1942, Ronald W. Harker, a test pilot with Rolls-Royce, flew a Mustang I and was favorably impressed with its performance up to medium altitudes. Harker also concluded that the Allison-powered Mustang was a disappointing performer at higher altitude. He told his superiors the fighter would perform even better with a Merlin 61. The "60 series" denoted two-stage, two-speed supercharged versions of the engine.

Lt. Col. Thomas (Tommy) Hitchcock, air attaché at the American embassy in London, was also report-

ing to Washington on the merits of the Merlin. The engine, according to Rolls-Royce engineers, could give the Mustang a maximum speed of 432mph (695km/h). Rolls-Royce's Ray Dorey, head of the engine flight-test section at Hucknall, steered Harker toward Air Chief Marshal Freemen, the Air Member for Production and Research, who arranged for three Mustang Is to be sent to Hucknall for installation of the improved Merlin 65. The first aircraft (AL975), designated Mustang Mk X, made its first flight on 13 October 1942 with Capt. R. T. Shepherd, Rolls-Royce chief test pilot, at the controls. The second ship (AL963) flew on 13 November 1942, the third (AM121) on 13 December.

Hitchcock reported the success of early Merlin test flights to the USAAF brass and to NAA officials. An American version of the Merlin was developed by Packard as the V-1650, and this engine powered the next production version of the NAA fighter.

The designation XP-78 was briefly applied to the re-engined Mustang with the Packard-built Merlin. Before any were actually built, the aircraft was redesignated P-51B.

Double Trouble is an operational P-51D Mustang of the 343rd FS/55th FG and has already claimed four Luftwaffe aircraft, as evidenced by the "kill" markings beneath the cockpit. The mirror attached to the sliding bubble canopy was found on some operational P-51Ds in the ETO. *Rockwell*

P-51B Model

The first of two XP-51B fighters (41-37352 and 41-37421), retaining the basic airframe but powered by a 1,450hp Packard V-1650-3 Merlin first flew for 45min on 30 November 1942, piloted by Chilton. It was found that a chemical reaction between different metals in the cooling system and the glycol coolant was clogging the radiator. A new radiator design and scoop were fitted to the second ship (41-37421), which proved free of the problem and performed well.

The P-51B went into production with the USAAF ordering 400 and Britain over a thousand, of which just 25 (FB100/124) were in due course delivered to the RAF as the Mustang Mk III. North American Aviation, which had never previously built a fighter, was now getting more business than it could handle. The company's Dallas, Texas, plant was chosen as a second outlet for the Mustang to build aircraft identical to the P-51B, which were designated P-51C (company NA-103).

The first P-51B (43-12093), or company NA-102, flew on 5 May 1943 with Chilton again as pilot. The first P-51C (42-102979) took to the air in August 1943 at Dallas. A total of 1,350 C models came from the Dallas factory altogether, and 944 P-51B/Cs became Mustang Mk IIIs with the RAF.

The Mustang design was now close to a level of maturity that would back the claim that it was the finest fighter to come out of World War II. Steady improvement of every facet of the airplane's design, from radiator to supercharger, from armament to electrical systems, had produced a better and better fighter. There remained one final change to create the definitive Mustang: the bubble canopy. As happened with the Thunderbolt, the flush canopy was discarded and the bubble adopted instead, itself the result of research that had developed the plastic bom-

bardier's nose on Army bombers. The "razorback" aft fuselage was cut down level with the fuselage forward section and the bubble installed. A dorsal fin was added to correct some minor stability problems that had come with the Merlin engine.

Two P-51Bs (43-12101/12102) were taken from the assembly line and converted into "proof of concept" vehicles for the P-51D, although they retained camouflage and lacked the dorsal fin. In the first of these, referred to at the time as an XP-51D, Chilton made the first flight of a bubble-canopy Mustang at Inglewood on 17 November 1943. Two prototype P-51D aircraft (company NA-106) from Inglewood (42-106539/106540) also came from the P-51B line.

With its armament, the P-51D solved what had been a nagging problem. Because the four .50cal (12.7mm) guns of earlier Mustangs had been mounted on their sides and tended to jam, the six guns in the P-51D were installed upright. The P-51D also carried more rounds per gun than previous models. Each inboard gun had 400 rounds, the four outboard guns 270. This was still not a lot, and pilots had to keep in mind that they were equipped with, at most, enough machine-gun bullets to fire for a few seconds. The lengthy bursts depicted in Hollywood films are unrealistic.

The first large P-51D production order, known by the company designation NA-109, constituted some 2,500 aircraft. The company designation NA-110 went to 100 similar ships that went to Australia for assembly by Commonwealth Aircraft Corporation. The manufacturer's terms NA-111, NA-122, and NA-124 covered further contracts for P-51D production that altogether totaled 6,502 airplanes built in Inglewood and 1,454 built at Dallas. These numbers include photo-reconnaissance ships that became known as the F-6D.

The P-51E designation was not assigned.

P-51F, G, and J

Though the Mustang was a thoroughbred from the start, almost from its inception engineers and pilots spoke of creating a lighter-weight version. A fair amount of funding and design work went into this effort. The real impetus, as with the original design, came from the British.

Little recognition has been bestowed, however, on the resulting XP-51F, XP-51G, and XP-51J lightweight fighters—even though they had so many internal differences that they resembled other Mustangs only in a superficial way. These F, G, and J model Mustangs, a total of seven airframes all known by the company designation NA-105, came into existence because NAA designer Edgar Schmued traveled to England and inspected Supermarine factories, as well as captured Messerschmitts and Focke-Wulfs.

The lightweight Mustang test ships were then built to a British specification. The simple logic was that less weight, with all other factors including engine horsepower remaining the same, would mean a faster ship, as well as improved performance in other areas.

The first flight of the XP-51F was made by Bob Chilton on 14 February 1944. Three were built (43-43332/43334). One of them was posed for portraits for record purposes on 10 April, although the pictures apparently were not released until later.

The XP-51F was powered by a 1,380hp Packard-built Rolls-Royce V-1650-3, the ubiquitous Merlin, driving a three-blade Aeroproducts propeller, and was described by Chilton as the best-performing fighter in the Mustang series. Coated with pounds of Simonize wax, the XP-51F attained 493mph (793km/h), but the magic 500mph (805km/h) figure proved frustratingly beyond reach.

Since the intent was to test the redesigned, light-weight airframe with several powerplants, the XP-51G followed, propelled by another Merlin, an imported 1,430hp Rolls-Royce RM-145M.

The first flight of the XP-51G appears to be a matter of some dispute. Most sources say the maiden flight was made 10 August 1944 by Edward Virgin, who later directed NAA operations in Washington, DC. A document from the manufacturer, however, credits Chilton with the first flight on 12 August while Paul Coggan (below) tells us that pilot Joe Barton may have achieved this honor on 9 August.

Two XP-51Gs were built (43-43335/43336). The second ship went to Boscombe Down and flew with the RAF as FR410. British priorities apparently had changed, however, and the fate of FR410 is unclear after the end of test flying in February 1945. The first XP-51G, fitted with a five-blade Dowty Rotol propeller, was used only once on a 20min flight and deemed a failure. Contrary to what most sources have told the world, all other flying was carried out with more conventional Aeroproducts Unimatic A-542-B1 four-blade props.

Remarkably, this first, very rare XP-51G fighter has survived. The book *Mustang Survivors* by Paul A. Coggan (Bourne Hill: Aston, 1987) tells us of efforts in the 1980s by John Morgan of La Canada, California, to restore and fly 43-43335. Morgan's task was not easy, for the XP-51G has parts not interchangeable with heavier, mass-produced Mustangs. It also has a different center of gravity.

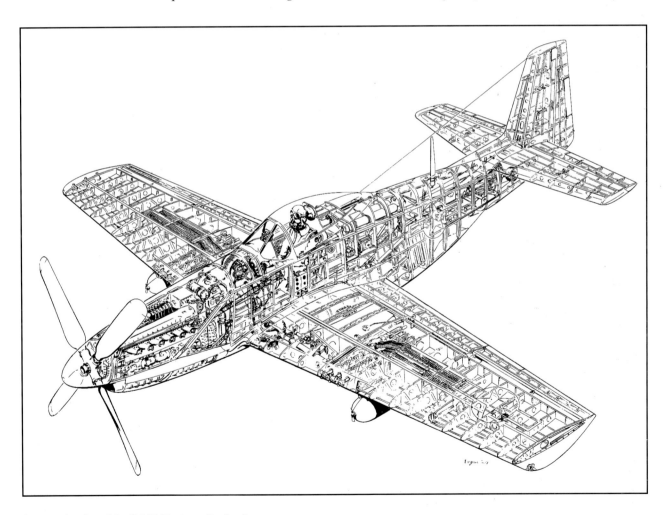

Cutaway drawing of the P-51D Mustang. *Rockwell*

A gap seems to have intervened before NAA completed the final model in this lightweight trio of Mustangs. Two XP-51Js (44-76027/76028) bring to seven the total of these lightweights. Maiden flight of the XP-51J was made on 23 April 1945 by Joe Barton, who flew most of the American tests with all three lightweights. Barton, incidentally, rarely receives credit for his major role in Mustang testing. Powerplant was the previously discarded 1,460hp Allison V-1710-119 with water injection.

After the war, Bob Chilton was asked why no in-flight photos of the XP-51F, XP-51G, and XP-51J have survived. Chilton said that, to his knowledge, none were taken. Pilots and others were too busy with testing programs to schedule photo sessions. In later years, NAA's Gene Boswell searched for a photographic record of these experimental lightweight Mustangs in the air, but his search was in vain.

While the lightweight Mustangs were not superior in every aspect of mission performance—they were not as easy to maintain and they were ill-equipped to operate from rough airfields—the XP-51F, G, and J out-performed other Mustangs. In time, they led to a production ship that incorporated

mature thinking on how to build a lightweight Mustang.

P-51H

The P-51H Mustang (company NA-126), powered by a 1,380hp V-1660-9A Merlin with water injection looked very good to Army planers, who placed an early order for a block of 2,400. The total eventually manufactured was 555.

First flight of a P-51H (44-64160) was made by Chilton at Inglewood on 3 February 1945. Though the H model, too, faced early directional stability problems that were resolved with minor changes, the P-51H might have become a formidable part of the American arsenal had a final invasion of Japan proven necessary. The P-51H was faster in level flight and in a dive than other Mustangs. In fact, with the ability to brush up close to the landmark speed of 500mph (805km/h) under certain circumstances, it was possibly the fastest propeller-driven fighter ever to attain operational service. Though it never saw combat, the H model served valiantly with Air Force and Air National Guard (ANG) squadrons in the postwar years.

Reconnaissance versions of the Mustang came off the production line together with P-51 fighters. F-6K Mustang 44-12813 of the 10th TRS, 69th TRG, is posing in the grass at Haguenau, France, in the fall of 1945. Note camera portal at the bottom rear fuselage just below the national insignia. *via Norman Taylor*

This lightweight NAA P-51H Mustang (44-64154) is on a proving flight near the manufacturer's plant in southern California. The P-51H never got into combat in World War II, contrary to some published reports (though a few reached Alaska before V-J Day), and the H model was not considered numerous enough to be practical for the war zone when the Korean conflict came along in 1950. Still, H model Mustangs served valiantly in the USAF and in National Guard squadrons.

P-51K and F-6K

Our narrative has already covered the XP-51J aircraft. The P-51K designation went to 1,335 Mustangs from the Dallas plant, identical to the P-51D but for a different propeller. Included in this total are 163 photo-reconnaissance versions, designated F-6K.

The P-51L (company NA-129) was to have been a Dallas-built Mustang identical to the P-51H model. 1,700 P-51Ls were ordered but the contract was canceled before any could be built or flown. A further variant from Inglewood, the P-51M (company NA-

124) with a V-1650-9A engine. One of these was built (the final P-51D, redesignated) and 1,628 subsequently canceled.

P/F-82 Twin Mustang

Long after the war was over, NAA built an aircraft that looked like a pair of Mustangs joined together by a single wing. The first of two XP-82 Twin Mustangs or company NA-120s (44-83886/83887), flown on 16 June 1945 by Joe Barton and Edward Virgin, was in nearly all respects a new aircraft. Its twin fuselages were not those of the P-51H, as widely reported, but of the XP-51F. These two "X" ships were the only Twin Mustangs powered by Packard V-1650-23/25 Merlin engines with counterrotating propellers. They were followed by the sole XP-82A (44-82888), which brought back the Allison V-1710 powerplant with common rotation.

The Twin Mustang resulted from a compelling need. The P-51 had extraordinary range. The P-51

This rare cutaway photo shows the XP-51J lightweight fighter, one of three bantam models (with the XP-51F and XP-51G) that performed well in tests but did not enter production. Two XP-51Js (44-76027/76028) were built but are rarely depicted in photos. First flight of the XP-51J was made on 23 April 1945 by company test pilot Joe Barton. Power was provided by the previously discarded 1,460hp Allison V-1710 engine, with the addition of water injection. *Rockwell*

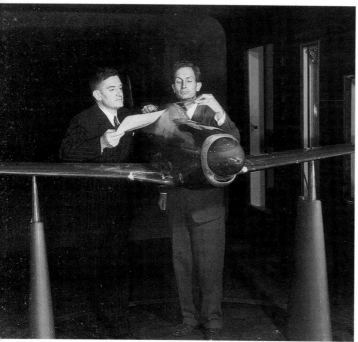

Edgar Schmued (left, overseeing work on a wind tunnel model) was the designer of the P-51 Mustang and head of the engineering team that made the fighter a reality. There will always be dispute over the extent to which the Mustang's designers did, or perhaps did not, make use of material on the P-40 and XP-46 they purchased from Curtiss-Wright. Schmued always insisted that a box of XP-46 material was ignored and that design of the Mustang was a wholly independent effort. *Rockwell*

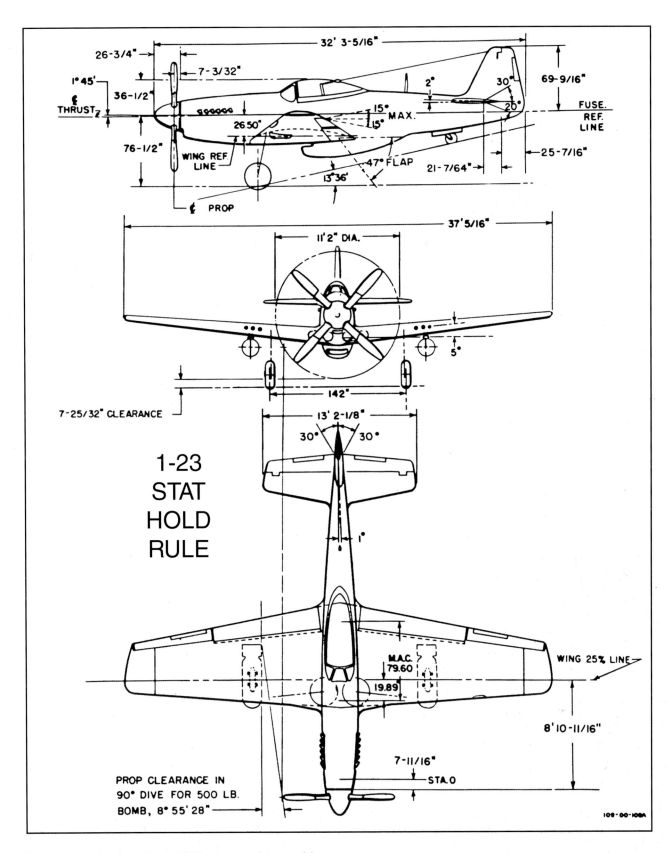

1-23
STAT
HOLD
RULE

This three-view drawing of the P-51D Mustang reveals many of the dimensions of this famous fighter, including its generous 142in main-wheel track. *Rockwell*

An entirely separate topic from our story of operational Mustangs is the large number of P-51s that have entered the civilian registry and have been flown as "warbirds" or for other duties. N2251D is one of several aircraft used by North American's (later Rockwell's) famous pilot Bob Hoover to demonstrate airplane handling qualities with exciting demonstrations at air shows. As with many civil Mustangs, this one has an extra seat added. *Rockwell*

could fly escort from England to deep into the Third Reich and over Czechoslovakia, northern Italy, and Poland. But this was not enough: even greater range was required for the final campaign against the Japanese home islands. The P-82 with twin engines, two pilots, and a huge fuel capacity was the answer. Later versions transformed the second crew member, on the starboard side of the Twin Mustang, into a radar operator.

Testing of three prototypes led to a USAAF order for 500 P-82B fighters, covered by company orders NA-123, but only 20 of these (44-65160/65179) were completed when the war ended. Two of these, also company NA-123s, were finished as night fighters designated P-82C (4465169) and P-82D (44-65170), with SCR-720 and APS-4 radar respectively.

In 1946, the USAAF placed an order for 100 P-82F or company NA-144 escort fighters (46-255/354), 100 P-82F or company NA-150 night fighters (46-405/504) with APS-4 radar, and 50 P-82G (46-355/404)

night fighters with SRC-720 radar.

The US Air Force (USAF) became an independent service branch on 18 September 1947. On 11 June 1948, the "P" for "pursuit" designation was changed to "F" for "fighter." The Mustang was now the F-51. The Twin Mustang became the F-82. Photo-reconnaissance Mustangs (the F-6 series) became RF-51s.

The only aircraft in our story that began life as a "fighter" rather than a pursuit ship was the F-82H, the final version of the Twin Mustang. This designation applied to the last nine P-82Fs (46-496/504) and five selected P-82Gs (46-384/388) that were "winterized" for service in Alaska. From the first P-82E onward, all Twin Mustangs were powered by 1,600hp Allison V-1710-143/145 engines with counterrotating props.

F-82F and F-82G Twin Mustangs were operated by Air Defense Command as interceptors, replacing the P-61B/C Black Widow. The F-82E served as a long-range escort with Strategic Air Command from 1948 to 1950. F-82Gs and F-82Hs served in the Korean War (chapter five) as, of course, did F-51D and RF-51D Mustangs.

In the 1950s, Temco Aircraft received a contract to convert 15 F-51D Mustangs into two-seat conversion trainers, designated TF-51D. In World War II, a number of Mustangs were converted to dual controls in the field by enterprising fighter squadron mechanics.

The Temco aircraft differed in having two distinct cockpits, separated by a center console, as well as a full set of dual instruments and controls.

In 1967, the USAF ordered an additional batch of Mustangs from Cavalier Aircraft Corp., which acquired design rights from NAA. These aircraft were intended for delivery to South American and Asian nations through the Military Assistance Program but were delivered in American markings with new serial numbers (67-14862/14866; 67-22579/22582; 72-1536/1541). Rebuilt from existing airframes, they were fitted with V-1650-7 engines, new radios, the tall P-51H-style fin, and a strengthened wing.

In 1968, the US Army employed a vintage F-51D (44-72990) as a chase aircraft for the YAH-56 Cheyenne battlefield helicopter. It was so successful, the Army ordered two Cavalier F-51Ds (68-15795/15796) as chase aircraft. Following the end of the Cheyenne program, these Mustangs were briefly used for other purposes and one (68-15795) was fitted with a 106mm recoilless rifle and used to evaluate the weapon's value in attacking fortified ground targets.

In 1968, Cavalier flight-tested a modified F-51 as the Turbo-Mustang III, powered by a 1,740shp Rolls-Royce Dart 510 turboprop engine. A similar conversion was toyed with, the following year, in Australia (see chapter 4) but no Dart-powered Mustang ever proved successful.

Two other Mustangs were converted with 2,455shp Lycoming T55-L-9 engines. This version was known as the Enforcer and made its first flight on 19 April 1971, the same year Piper Aircraft acquired design rights from Cavalier. Tests of these aircraft in the early 1970s failed to arouse much interest on the part of USAF officers, but Congress kept pushing the Enforcer, anyway. In September 1981, a contract was placed with Piper for two new-build PA-48 Enforcer airframes, the first of which made its maiden flight on 9 April 1983. The USAF evaluated the two PA-48 prototypes exhaustively before retiring them from flight status in 1986. Barely recognizable as Mustangs, the two "new build" Enforcers are included in our total for aircraft manufactured, while the two converted aircraft (which did not acquire new serials) are not.

This overview of the Mustang story sets the stage. Now, the curtain rises on the Mustang in combat.

The very last operational user of the P-51 Mustang in the US military was the US Army, which employed this F-51D (44-72990) as a chase aircraft for the AH-56 Cheyenne advanced helicopter program. The Army Mustang is seen at Edwards Air Force Base, California, in July 1968. *via Jim Sullivan*

CHAPTER 2

P-51 Mustang at War

The sleek Mustang I fighter reached embattled British pilots shortly after the RAF fielded its Army Co-Operation Command (ACC), equipped with fighter-bombers to support ground-pounding soldiers. ACC's principal tool in January 1942 was the Curtiss Tomahawk IIA, roughly equivalent to the P-40D. As ACC's squadrons went into action over France, the Tomahawk IIA proved too vulnerable when engaged by enemy fighters. When No. 26 Squadron at Gatwick took delivery of its first Mustang Is in that first month of 1942, British pilots finally had the means to snap back and fight for real if they were bounced by Messerschmitt Bf 109s.

Number 241 Squadron at Bottisham and No. 268 Squadron at Weston Zoyland followed, becoming operational in the lean, powerful Mustang I. These were followed in mid-1942 by seven more RAF squadrons (Nos. 63, 169, 170, 171, 408, 400, and 414).

Pilots of No. 26 Squadron carried out the first Mustang sortie over occupied Europe, a reconnaissance mission, on 5 May 1942.

For weeks to come, pilots were instructed to disengage if attacked and bring their reconnaissance findings home. The lack of an air-to-air "test" was rectified on 19 August 1942 when Mustang Is supported Operation Jubilee, the Anglo-Canadian landings at Dieppe.

Dieppe put the Allies in direct challenge to Luftwaffe squadrons throughout France and the Low Countries. Among five dozen combat squadrons in action in conjunction with the disastrous Dieppe raid, four flew Mustangs—Nos. 26, 239, 400 (RCAF), and 414 (RCAF). A catastrophic 106 RAF aircraft were lost on that day, among them ten Mustangs. Pilot Officer Hollis H. Hills' FW 190 kill was almost the only good news. Hills was an American who'd enlisted in the RCAF before Pearl Harbor.

Army Co-Operation Command was not a comfortable place to be in 1942. No fewer than 40 Mustangs were lost by the RAF during the remainder of the year. The vulnerability of any liquid-cooled war-plane to ground fire, a drawback that will recur throughout the Mustang story, contributed to the losses. As 1943 began, British Mustangs continued their fight over the continent and on occasion drew blood from their German adversaries.

Mustang in Combat

The first air-to-air victory for the Mustang was racked up in British colors during the star-crossed Dieppe raid on 19 August 1942, when an American in the RAF, Pilot Off. Hollis H. Hills, shot down a Focke-Wulf FW 190. On that day, Hills' No. 2 Squadron also lost a Mustang, the first to go down in battle.

While Hills went on to achieve five aerial victories and become the first Mustang ace (on 11 June 1943), the debut of the Mustang in American livery took place on 9 April 1943 when a 154th Observation Squadron F-6A aircraft piloted by Lt. Alfred Schwab carried out a successful reconnaissance mission. On 23 April 1943, a Mustang from the same squadron was shot down in error by Allied gun batteries—the first American Mustang lost in the war.

Also in April 1943, A-36 Apaches went with the 27th Fighter-Bomber Group (FBG) to Rasel Ma, French Morocco, where the Allies were pressing the all-important North Africa campaign. On 6 June 1943, A-36 dive bombers accompanied a strike on the island of Pantelleria. The 86th Fighter Group (FG) picked up the attack version of the Mustang soon thereafter.

Halfway around the world, the 311th FG went into combat in the fall of 1943, using the A-36 to cover

43-12201 is a flush-canopy P-51B Mustang of the kind that was widely in service in USAAF combat squadrons before the sleeker, bubble-canopy P-51D came along. Of interest is the US national insignia that was in use only briefly, only from June to August, 1943. It was determined that the "surround" of Insignia Red might, from a distance, be mistaken for the red of the Japanese *hinomaru*, or "meatball." The border was replaced by one of Insignia Blue that is still in use today. *Rockwell*

The 206th Mustang Mark I for the RAF (AG550, coded U-XV) poses on a misleadingly calm flight over English countryside, in about 1942, when the situation was anything but serene. Evident in this view is the air scoop above the cowl, a trademark of Allison-powered Mustangs. The RAF was responsible for the Mustang design to begin with but never really used the fighter to its full potential, employing Mustangs mostly for Army cooperation duties. This meant the air-to-ground mission, for which the Mustang was less well suited than it was for air-to-air combat. *RAF*

Allied operations along the Ledo Road in Burma. The 311th also had a few Allison-powered P-51A aircraft. According to number crunchers, A-36s flew 23,373 combat sorties and dropped 16,000,000 pounds of bombs in the China-Burma-Indonesia region. Though supposedly not an air-to-air combatant, the A-36 also shot down 84 Japanese aircraft.

In due course, the 311th traded its Allison-powered dive bombers and fighters for Merlin-powered P-51Bs. The 23rd FG, which traced its lineage to Gen. Claire Chennault's "Flying Tigers" and continued to wear a shark's mouth on each of its aircraft, also received Merlin-powered P-51B Mustangs.

The war in China was a long, difficult slog for the Fourteenth Air Force which picked up more and more Mustangs as the war progressed. The 23rd FG's top-scoring Mustang pilot was Col. John (Pappy) Herbst who eventually claimed 18 Japanese warplanes.

The Mustang later became so important as an escort for Allied bombers that it's worth remembering the P-51's best-known mission evolved gradually. As the bombing campaign over Europe grew, the Eighth Air Force in England looked at disturbing losses of four-engine bombers and assigned high priority to a need it had earlier identified, the need for a long-range fighter to escort the bombers and duel with the Germans' superb Messerschmitts and Focke-Wulfs. The need was graphically illustrated by the 17 August 1943 Schweinfurt-Regensburg raid on which 60 out of 376 bombers were lost, a disturbing 16 percent of the total force.

Escort Mission

Eighth Air Force chief Lt. Gen Ira C. Eaker was determined to continue the bombing offensive against the Third Reich but was equally convinced that a way had to be found to offer better protection to the bombers. After a period of laying low, Eaker's bombers took to the skies again only to have the situation worsen in a dramatic way. In a single week (8–14 October 1943) during raids on Bremen, Marienburg, Danzig, and Munster, no fewer than 148 bombers and 1,500 crew members were lost. Then came Black Thursday, the 14 October 1943 raid when 60 out of 280 bombers were shot down, 20 percent of the entire force.

30

EV998 is apparently one of 944 P-51B and P-51C aircraft that were delivered to the British as Mustang Mark IIIs. The air-to-ground mission earmarked for the British warplanes is evident here with two box-finned bombs, which appear to be 1,000lb (454 kilogram), and with the aircraft's extended, "bread slicer" speed brakes like those on the American A-36 Apache. The British were the first to learn, the hard way, that it was not always prudent to attack a ground target in a plane with a coolant device located amidships at the bottom of the fuselage. The device was dreadfully vulnerable to even a glancing hit by a bullet or shrapnel. *RAF*

The Eighth sent Col. Cass Hough, head of its technical section, to test-fly the P-51B. He reported back on the Mustang's many qualities and its enormous potential but also said that directional stability problems needed to be fixed. After the P-51D with teardrop canopy and dorsal fin came along, no one worried about problems any more.

The Merlin-powered Mustang had significantly better fuel consumption than other Allied fighters. The final change that had to be made was to install an 85gal fuel tank behind the pilot. As so often happens, a benefit in one area of performance led to a problem in another. The added fuel tank exacerbated the directional stability problem to the extent that for the first hour or two on a mission, the pilot would have to concentrate very hard on keeping flying the way the nose was pointing. By then, the extra tank would be

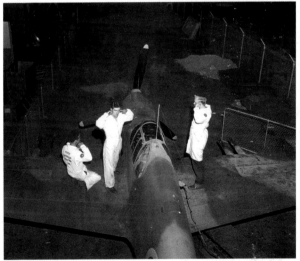

For the Mustang to succeed in combat, its guns had to be bore-sighted, properly maintained, and repeatedly tested. This British Mustang Mark I (possibly AG348, the fourth aircraft built) is getting a noisy, nocturnal trial of its lethal four 20mm cannons. From this angle, it's evident that the earliest canopy shape of the Mustang afforded the pilot very little visibility to the rear, making it necessary for him to weave in order to check out his vulnerable six o'clock position. Although this night firing is taking place at the North American plant, similar shooting rehearsals were performed regularly in the combat zone. *North American Aviation*

The view of a P-51B Mustang that no Luftwaffe pilot ever wanted to see behind him, closing in and ready to fire. This angle accentuates the very thin frontal silhouette of the fighter, which tended to reduce the Mustang's vulnerability to gunfire under some circumstances. *North American Aviation*

empty and the pilot could switch to the usual 184gal tanks in the wings, his directional stability problem solved.

With two 75gal drop tanks under the wings, the Mustang needed a long, nerve-wracking takeoff roll and could only just stagger into the sky, but when the entire fuel load was added up (419gal), this fighter had now become a long-legged demon. Test pilot Col. Mark Bradley flew one from Inglewood down to Albuquerque, spent some time loitering around in the air over New Mexico's largest city, and then, without landing, returned to the factory. The significance of this little jaunt over the southwest was that Bradley had just done the equivalent of England to Berlin and back!

Surprisingly, the first Merlin-powered P-51Bs to become operational in England belonged not to the Eighth Air Force, which needed them for bomber escort, but to the Ninth Air Force, which was charged with air-to-ground combat responsibilities to support the expected invasion of occupied Europe.

The 354th FG at Boxsted under Lt. Col. Kenneth Martin was the first unit in the European Theater of Operations (ETO) to receive Mustangs, the first arrivals being P-51Bs. The group, consisting of the 353rd, 355th, and 356th Fighter Squadrons (FS), remained under the jurisdiction of Ninth Air Force but was immediately ordered to support bomber operations.

In the Mustang's first combat mission by an American fighter group, an 11 December 1943 bomber escort to Emden, not much happened. A few days later, Lt. Charles F. Gumm shot down a twin-engine Messerschmitt Bf 110 for the first aerial victory by an American Mustang group. Gumm's success was overshadowed by the loss of Maj. Owen M. Seaman, commander of the 353rd FS, who vanished over the North Sea. By the end of the month, the 354th FG had shot down eight Luftwaffe aircraft, including four more rocket-carrying Bf 110s but had lost eight

Previously unpublished study of a P-51B Mustang (42-106812) that has returned from a combat mission in the ETO with rather severe battle damage. The right wing of the aircraft has been punched open in numerous places. Note the Normandy "invasion" stripes and the RAF Lockheed Hudson bomber in the background. The full story is not known, but it appears the damaged Mustang is now receiving a once-over from its dedicated crew chief, who will want to put it back into action. *Warren M. Bodie*

Don't know where, don't know when . . . Never before published, this slightly faded view of a razorback Mustang nicknamed *Dot* seems to illustrate the A-36 Apache version, and for some reason it seems to be in the CBI theater, but there's no other information that can be located. Perhaps a reader will know something about the bombing missions signified by the light-colored silhouettes located beneath the stacks for the Allison engine. *via Nick Veronico*

Mustangs, most due to technical problems. While this was going on, the group's pilots were adjusting to what amounted to a new kind of warfare. Now, the Mustang pilots were facing 4–5hr missions. This kind of flying imposed new demands on the pilot, creating all kinds of discomfort, but it was even worse on the airplane. The Mustang was prone to coolant loss at high altitude where engines overheated and eventually seized. Coolant, oil, and oxygen problems needed to be resolved.

Arrival of Mustangs with Eighth Air Force units in Britain gave the Allies a tremendous boost in their aerial campaign against Hitler's *Festung Europa*, or Fortress Europe. Whatever Lightning or Jug pilots might have said then, or might say today with a half-century of hindsight, the Mustang's combination of speed and maneuverability was superior to other U.S. fighters and it had the "legs" to go deep into enemy territory.

Medal Mission

On 11 January 1944, Maj. James H. Howard of the 354th repeatedly risked his life to defend bombers from Luftwaffe fighter attack. Separated from his flight, Howard was alone near a B-17 bomber formation that came under attack from six to eight twin-engine German fighters. There were at least dozens of Luftwaffe fighters not far away. Howard unhesitatingly went into harm's way and shot down, in quick succession, a twin-engine ship, an FW 190, and a Bf

109. Moments later, he shook another Bf 109 off the tail of an American aircraft. Howard continued fighting aggressive and persistent Luftwaffe pilots for a half-hour thereafter. His ship during the engagement was 43-6315, nicknamed *Ding Hao!*. A soft-spoken figure who wrote up a report of the incident without mention of his own heroism, Howard received the highest American award for valor, the Medal of Honor.

The 357th FG, also assigned to the Ninth Air Force but released to operational control of the Eighth for bomber escort, flew its first P-51B Mustang mission on 11 February 1944, with Major Howard (on loan from the 354th) in the lead.

On 23 February 1944, the 363rd FG became the third P-51B Mustang operator in the European theater, flying from Rivenhall. That same month, the 4th FG at Debden, under Col. Donald Blakeslee, also began converting to the P-51B.

Blakeslee was chosen to lead his fighters to Berlin on 3 March 1944, but fate threw a monkey wrench into his prospect of being first over the Third Reich's capital. Blakeslee's 4th FG, which included the 334th, 335th, and 336th squadrons, set forth but were recalled en route because of deteriorating weather. P-38 Lightnings of the 55th FG under Lt. Col. Jack Jenkins failed to receive the recall and continued on to Berlin, becoming the first Allied fighters to do so. A second attempt to take P-51Bs to Berlin was also fouled by the weather but on 6 March 1944, Blakeslee led his Mustangs into a furious battle over the capital. That month, the 4th FG claimed 156 Luftwaffe aircraft destroyed.

By the spring of 1944, five more fighter groups in the Eighth Air Force (339th, 352nd, 355th, 359th, and 361st) were equipping with P-51B/C Mustangs.

On 1 March 1944, 1st Lt. Charles Gumm of the 355th FS/354th FG was killed after crash-landing his Mustang, which had experienced engine trouble on takeoff. Gumm, as one of the first Mustang pilots, had enormous potential, and his loss was deeply felt.

The Med

In the Mediterranean theater, Mustang maintenance crews, crew chiefs, and pilots struggled with moisture and mud, even when relatively sunny skies prevailed. The 31st and 52nd FGs, which had flown Spitfire Mk Vs in North Africa, took delivery of P-51D Mustangs in Italy in April 1944. The 325th FG followed. The 31st flew its first big mission on 21 April

It was not unusual for fighters in the CBI theater to be far less colorful than those flying over Europe. Not much of anything in the way of distinctive markings is evident on this P-51B Mustang seen at Tingkawk SeKan, Burma, in July 1944. Men fighting in the CBI felt themselves "neglected" and often received equipment more slowly than those in Europe, but the Mustang made its contribution here, as elsewhere. *Warren M. Bodie*

Beautifully preserved at the Eighth Air Force Museum, Barksdale AFB, Louisiana, under the ministrations of curator Buck Rigg, this aircraft is not an identifiable Mustang at all but a collection of com-ponents from several Mustangs. It's restored to represent *Ridge Runner*, a bubble-canopy P-51D flown by air ace Maj. Pierce W. McKennon of the 4th FG.

Introduction of the bubble-canopy P-51D Mustang was the final step to full maturity for North American's incomparable fighter design. This previously unpublished view depicts *Silver Streak*, the P-51D Mustang flown by 1st Lt. Dan Leftwich of the 384th FS/364th FG in the ETO. Leftwich was credited with four and one-half Focke-Wulf FW 190s, including two in a single day in December 1944. *via Dan Leftwich*

1944, when its Mustangs escorted B-24s attacking the oil refineries at Ploesti, Romania.

The first RAF squadron in Italy to equip with Mustangs was No. 260, which received Mustang IIIs at Cutella in April 1944.

The red-tailed 332nd FG, which shifted from the Thunderbolt to the P-51D Mustang in June 1944 at Lesina, Italy, was the only pursuit ship outfit in the entire, segregated Army to have pilots who were called Negroes then and are known today as African-Americans. Lee A. Archer was the group's top-scoring ace with five and six ground victories. One day, Archer and Wendell O. Pruitt went rushing into a formation of Messerschmitts that outnumbered them six to one. Each American scored two kills and came through the fight unharmed.

In June 1944, the 10th Tactical Reconnaissance Group (TRG) picked up the 12th and 15th Tactical Reconnaissance Squadrons (TRS), equipped with F-6B and F-6C Mustang photo planes. The F-6s retained six .50cal (12.7mm) machine guns and frequently scrapped with Luftwaffe fighters. Capt. Clyde East of the 15th squadron became the war's top-scoring reconnaissance pilot with 15 aerial victories.

What looks like a "black hole" beneath the aft part of the national insignia is, in fact, a camera opening for this photo-reconnaissance version of the Mustang, an F-6K (44-12813). This ship belongs to the 10th TRS, part of the 69th TRG, and is seen at Haguneau, France, in 1945. Photo-recce versions of the Mustang carried guns and had a genuine combat role throughout the conflict. *via Norman Taylor*

Big Beautiful Doll was a P-51D Mustang (44-72218) flown by Lt. Col. John D. Landers, who commanded the 78th FG. The 78th was one of the last groups to take delivery of Mustangs as the war in Europe moved toward its conclusion. Landers added four and one-half aerial victories in the Mustang to four P-38 kills with the 55th FG and six P-40 kills in the Pacific to become one of the top-scoring American aces of the Second World War. He also destroyed 20 enemy aircraft on the ground. *Rockwell*

By D-Day, 6 June 1944, the German air arm was on the defensive, as much a dangerous foe as a cornered wildcat, but never again to hold air superiority in any engagement. The air-to-ground role remained dangerous, and the RAF lost three Mustang Mk Is on D-Day. One of these (AM225) from No. 168 Squadron exploded in mid-air over the English Channel and may have been hit by a shell from a bombarding warship.

Four RAF Mustang squadrons (Nos. 129, 306, 315, and 316) were assigned to defensive operations against the German V-1 buzz bomb threat. The V-1 represented a small and difficult target, especially when the fighters defending against it were often forced to maneuver over home territory where they were not free to fire at random. Moreover, the problem of merely finding an incoming V-1 was a difficult one. American Mustangs of the 354th FG also intercepted and destroyed a number of V-1s.

It should be noted that the 354th "Pioneer Mustang" group had plenty of other achievements to its credit. One pilot, Col. Jack T. Bradley, claimed he shot down two Bf 109s in just 10sec. The 354th produced the Ninth Air Force's top-scoring ace, 1st Lt. Glenn Eagleston, who racked up 18.5 victories (and later added two more to his score in Korea). Captain Don M. Beerbower, another 354th pilot, was close behind with 15.5.

The 4th FG claimed no fewer than 1,016 enemy aircraft destroyed in the air and on the ground during its years of combat using the Spitfire, P-47, and P-51. The 4th also produced its share of aces, including Capt. Donald S. Gentile with 21.8 kills and Capt. John T. Godfrey with 18.

Top Ace

The 352nd FG produced the top-scoring Mustang pilot of all, Maj. George E. Preddy, Jr., who was credited with 26.83 aerial victories and five aircraft destroyed on the ground.

In his painting *Checkmate*, Heinz Krebs recalls a triumphant low pass over an immobilized "target of opportunity" belonging to the Reichsbahn, the German state-owned railroad. It is 1945, the Mustang is being increasingly used against ground targets, and the pass is led by Lt. Col. John D. Landers of the 78th FG. Landers' plane *Big Beautiful Doll*, a P-51D Mustang (44-72218), is in the lead. Copies of this print, signed by four 78th FG aces, are available from Art-Haus, 6541 North Cibola Avenue, Tucson, Arizona 85718, telephone (602) 529-1432. *Heinz Krebs*

On 21 June 1944, the Eighth Air Force flew its first long-range "shuttle" bombing mission aimed at reaching targets in Germany that had previously been out of reach. This feat was accomplished by landing in Russia to refuel and rearm before attacking other targets on the way home. One hundred and sixty-three B-17 Flying Fortresses were escorted by 61 Mustangs of the 4th FG plus one squadron from the 352nd FG, all led by Col. Don Blakeslee.

By the summer of 1944, rapidly arriving P-51Ds were in command of the air. Although the very top-ranking American aces in Europe flew P-47 Thunderbolts, the Mustang was the aircraft of many air aces whose mastery over the Luftwaffe made their names familiar to a generation of aviation followers—Lt.

Col. John C. Meyer with 24 air and 13 ground victories, Maj. George E. Preddy, Jr., with a tongue-twisting score of 26.83 enemy aircraft shot down plus five destroyed on the ground (the decimal figure was caused by more than one pilot sharing credit for the same kill), and Capt. Don S. Gentile with 21.83 air and six ground kills. Gentile, of course, cracked up an aircraft while "beating up" his own airfield, an incident that caused him to be sent packing. As with all such historical quirks, it is impossible to avoid wondering how Gentile might have fared, had he been able to complete his tour of duty.

This painting by 357th FG historian Merle Olmsted depicts: *Top*, P-51B Mustang 43-24823, 353rd FS, piloted by Bill Overstreet, credited with 2.5 aerial victories. Previously, the Mustang had been Clarence "Bud" Anderson's *Old Crow* until Anderson completed his combat tour. The insignia is a winged horse over a black mustang. *Center*, Noorduyn UC-64A Norseman 43-35444, *Spirit Of St. Louis*, was the 357th FG "hack" from November 1944 until the end of the war. *Bottom*, P-51D Mustang 44-13318, *Frenesi*, 364th FS, flown by squadron commander Lt. Col. Tommy Hayes (see chapter 3), wearing black and white Normandy invasion stripes on the rear fuselage. *Merle Olmsted*

The Mustang will never be forgotten as the "little friend" escort for bombers to Berlin. Halfway around the world on a piece of rock called Iwo Jima, P-51 pilots fought a different war. One by one, Mustangs roll down the dusty path from the parking area to the runway on Iwo. These bubble-canopy P-51D models belong to the 457th FS of the 506th FG. *USAF via Jeffrey L. Ethell*

The Axis was anything but ready to roll over and play dead the moment Mustangs appeared on the scene. On 28 July 1944, Mustang pilots of the 359th FG on an escort mission to Merseburg ran into the Me 163 rocket-propelled fighter for the first time. On 5 August 1944, Me 163s shot down three Mustangs with their 30mm cannons.

Captain George Preddy, Jr., of the 352nd FG set a record on 6 August 1944, claiming six aerial victories in a single fight, all of them Bf 109s. Not until 16 August, however, did Mustang pilots get in their licks against the strange and new Luftwaffe rocket aircraft, shooting down two Me 163s.

The Messerschmitt Me 262 was the world's first operational jet fighter. In the ETO, Eighth Air Force chief Gen. James E. Doolittle was seriously concerned about German jets and had to admit that there was very little he could do about the problem, except to

First Lieutenant Bill Overstreet, 353rd FS/357th FG stands beside the art work on his P-51B Mustang 43-24823. The insignia is a winged horse over a black mustang. *Merle Olmsted*

In second place behind a clump of trees at Gettysburg, the Iwo Jima summit of Mount Surabachi (center, background) is the costliest real estate ever assaulted by Americans. Following the 19 February 1945 invasion, *Jimmy* (44-63353), wearing plane-in-group number 124, plows through the sky ahead of *Sweet Rosalee* (44-72641), whose serial and plane-in-group number 104 are not readily visible. Beneath *Jimmy's* cockpit is the emblem of the 78th FS, approved on 14 September 1933 and described as a bushmaster's head on a blue disc with a wide yellow border. The emblem is reversed in comparison with the official version in order to face forward. The 78th was one of three squadrons in the 15th FG. Iwo Jima was invaded on 19 February 1945. *Jimmy* is a Dallas-built P-51D-NT while *Sweet Rosalee* is Los Angeles-manufactured P-51D-NA. *USAAF via Joseph H. Fahey*

increase the number of escort fighters per long-range mission over the continent.

On 28 August 1944, the first aerial victory over the Me 262 was racked up by Eighth Air Force P-47 Thunderbolt pilots over Belgium. On 7 October 1944, 1st Lt. Urban Drew of the 361st FG scored the first such kills for the Mustang, claiming two Me 262s as they were taking off from Achmer.

On 2 November 1944, Capt. William Cullerton of the 357th FS/355th FG and his flight chased four Me 262s away from US bombers and went on to down two Bf 109s in the air and destroy six more on the ground. A Mustang victory over the Me 262 was toted up on 6 November 1944 by Capt. Charles E. Yeager of the 357th FG, who earlier had downed five Luftwaffe aircraft in a single day.

Returning from escorting a formation of Flying Fortresses over Leuna on 8 November 1944, P-51D Mustang pilots Lts. James W. Kenney and Warren Corwin of the 357th Fighter Group spotted a Luftwaffe aircraft moving toward the B-17s and identified it as an Me-262. The jets had been thrown into action, and led, by Major Walter Nowotny, the 258-kill German ace and holder of the Knight's Cross.

The Mustang pilots saw the jet make a firing pass from ten o'clock to the bomber formation. Thereafter, the jet fighter made a surprisingly quick 180deg turn and prepared to come back for another pass from five o'clock. Kenney, with Corwin behind him, made a pass on the jet. Kenney began firing from about 400 yards and saw a puff of smoke belch forth from the Me 262.

The German pilot dove for the deck. Corwin flew a split-S to provide backup support while Kenney rolled down on the Me 262 and got on its tail again.

First Lieutenant William Spencer was a P-51D Mustang pilot with Col. Don Blakeslee's fabled 4th FG, flying from Debden, England. A member of the group's 334th FS, Spencer is seen in the cockpit with typical helmet and goggles for the well-dressed flyer of 1944 and also poses in front of his parked Mustang. *Bill Spencer*

Kenney overshot twice, demonstrating that the Mustang was not to be under-rated even in the presence of a jet, but the second time the Me 262 pilot went into a turn to the left and the American pilot was able to close in and score hits with his machine-guns. The German pilot, Capt. Franz Schall, bailed out, giving Kenney a memorable jet kill. A second Me 262 was claimed by another Mustang pilot in a separate action on the same day.

Preddy Loss

On 25 December 1944, Maj. George E. Preddy of the 328th FS/352nd FG shot down two Bf 109s near Koblenz. These were his 25th and 26th kills and qualified him as the seventh-ranking USAAF ace of the war. Preddy then pursued an FW 190 near Liege. The Focke-Wulf and the Mustang ran into heavy American machine gun fire from the ground. Preddy's Mustang was hit and his efforts to save himself were in vain. His fighter plunged into the ground and he was killed.

Thanks in no small measure to a series of blunders by the Germans, some of them caused by Hitler second-guessing his general staff, the Luftwaffe's growing fleet of jet fighters was not able to prevail over the persistent Allies, and the Mustang continued to rule the air. On the other side of the world, Japan fielded a few advanced prop-driven fighters before the end of the conflict, but no operational jets, and there was no serious challenge to American supremacy. But when it was all over, Americans were forced to admit that things could have happened differently.

The final RAF squadron to receive Mustangs during the war was No. 611, which began to re-equip in January 1945 at Hawkinge. The squadron received Mustang IV (P-51D) and Mustang IVA (P-51K) variants. As the war progressed into 1945 and Allied troops moved across Europe, No. 611 pilots encountered the enemy's exotic jet and rocket fighters in the air and on the ground.

In March 1945, jet fighter activity reached an unprecedented level with USAAF fighters reporting 438 encounters, 280 fights, and 43 Me 262 kills.

In the Pacific theater, the first Mustang to see service was the F-6D reconnaissance aircraft that began to replace P-40s with the 82nd TRS at Morotai in November 1944. In early 1945, the 35th and 348th FGs, then fighting in the Philippines, began to replace their weary Thunderbolts with P-51D Mustangs.

It was that tiny crag of rock, the island of Iwo Jima, invaded by US Marines on 19 February 1945 that eventually became home for a massive P-51 force. Mustangs of the 15th FG began arriving at Iwo Jima's South Field on 6 March 1945. The 23rd and 306th FGs followed. Soon P-51 Mustangs, usually carrying two 165gal drop tanks, began escorting B-29 Superfortresses in the final campaign against the Japanese home islands. In mid-May, the Mustang-equipped 506th FG joined the escort force on Iwo.

On 11 January 1945, Maj. William A. Shomo was at the controls of a P-51D Mustang (44-72505), the *Fly-*

A previously unpublished glimpse of a tropical interlude. At Mokolea in the Hawaiian Islands, members of the 72nd FS/21st FG stand beside a P-51D Mustang (44-63409) wearing the group's distinctive markings, which include dark blue stripes on wings, elevator, and rear fuselage. It is early 1945, and the 21st is soon to move to Iwo Jima to become one of four fighter groups fighting from several airfields on that hard-won island. *Bill Bradbury*

ing Undertaker (named for his truncated civilian career as a mortician and not an F-6D reconnaissance ship as is often reported) on a mission over northern Luzon in the Philippines. Attacked by a swarm of Japanese fighters including Ki-44 (Tojo) and Ki-61 (Tony) fighters, Shomo pulled off the unprecedented feat of shooting down seven Japanese warplanes in a single mission. For this achievement, he became the second Mustang pilot of World War II to be awarded the Medal of Honor.

The Mustang was a bit of a latecomer to the war, but it eventually became an almost universal sight. The best-known groups (many of which used earlier fighters at an earlier stage in the war and finished with Mustangs) are:

In the Mediterranean theater of operations: the 31st, 52nd, 325th, and 332nd FGs.

In the ETO: the 4th, 20th, 55th, 78th, 339th, 352nd, 353rd, 354th, 355th, 356th, 357th, 359th, 361st, 364th, 370th, and 479th FGs.

In the China-Burma-India (CBI) theater and in the Pacific: 1st Air Commando Group, 3rd Air Commando Group, and the 15th, 21st, 23rd, 33rd, 35th, 51st, 306th, 311th, 348th, and 506th FGs.

In addition, the 27th and 86th FBG in the Mediterranean and the 311th FBG in India employed the A-36 Apache. Numerous American units employed F-6A through F-6G photo-reconnaissance versions of the Mustang.

In the RAF, Nos. 2, 19, 26, 65, 112, 122, 129, 213, 249, 260, 306, 315, 316, and 611 Squadrons were operators of the Mustang, among many others. Australia, New Zealand, and South Africa also flew the Mustang in combat.

In addition to Europe and the Pacific, P-51 Mustangs served with several USAAF groups in the CBI, where operating conditions were often primitive and it was always difficult to "keep 'em flying." In these views, P-51Ds wear the checkerboard tail markings of the 25th FS, the Assam Dragons, part of the 51st FG, and are seen at an airfield in China in 1945. *Duane E. Biteman*

Once the war was won, the P-51 Mustang became part of occupation forces. This P-51D (44-72161) was flown by 1st Lt. James Kunkle and was known as *Kunk's Klunk*. The Mustang is seen in Bremen, Germany, in 1946. This previously unpublished shot tells us that postwar fliers had to operate from pierced steel planking (PSP) in many locations, a kind of hurried solution to the destruction wreaked by Allied bombing. *Warren M. Bodie*

P-51D Mustang 44-64315 wearing rare, short-lived tail stripes at Selfridge Field, Michigan, in July 1946. This angle on the P-51H model shows the taller tail fin and semi-streamlined bomb pylons, which are quite different in appearance from the squared-off, brute-strength pylons employed on the Republic P-47 Thunderbolt. To set the record straight: although P-51H fighters were available to support the planned amphibious invasion of the Japanese home islands, the H model did *not* see combat in World War II. *Warren M. Bodie*

CHAPTER 3
Pilot Talk

On 2 March 1944, I shot down my first German aircraft. A flight of four Me 109s were sighted over Frankfurt at 23,000ft. When engaged, two broke off and were engaged by my element of two. My wingman, John Carder, and I met the lead pair head-on. It was two on two. The playing field was level with ample space above and below. A fair fight? Only the face-off! [Author's note: Throughout the war and for years afterward, Americans referred to the Messerschmitt Bf 109 as the Me 109 even though, as author Bill Gunston has said in reference to the year 1943, "we were drowning in Bf 109 nameplates by then."]

The Germans used all the air space and they flew their craft well as we jockeyed for position. When they dived for the deck they had played their last card. They could turn, climb, or run. None were viable options. They split and turned. With our greater speed and maneuverability they quickly "bought the farm" after a short burst from each of our sets of six .50cal guns. John and I returned to base, chalked up our victories, and savored the GI ration of whiskey.

It was quick. Almost textbook. It demonstrated the superiority of the P-51. For me it was fulfilling. It was exhilarating. What an aircraft!

To go back. On 7 December 1941, I was enjoying my last day with my bride of six months, now two months pregnant. The next morning I was to board an Army sea transport on a PCS [permanent change of station] move to the Philippines.

Pearl Harbor changed all that. The Army located 55 crated P-40s. Like numbers of pilots, crew chiefs, and armorers were assembled. All were loaded aboard the commandeered vessel *President Polk*. Also aboard was an antiaircraft unit from Texas.

It was a first-class cruise as the *Polk* had been scheduled to depart on 8 December on a round-the-world cruise. The plan was to sneak us into Mindanao or some southern island. One might say we did that after we stopped at Brisbane and assembled

our P-40s. We worked in shifts around the clock. The crew chiefs were in charge: they told the pilots what to do, like how to use a torque wrench. Most of us knew how to use a crow bar.

Veteran pilots had been sent down from the Philippines to lead the 55 who were yet to get their feet wet. They were a gung-ho group and dedicated to get back to the P. I. and get even. There was no way to get back. A secure base in Java was as far north as possible. As soon as 16 P-40s were flyable, they headed north through Darwin, Timor, Bali, to Surabaya. The first group left in mid-January, all were assigned to the 17th Pursuit Squadron (Provisional). Major Sprague and his colleagues from the P.I.—which had not fallen to the Japanese—were the flight and element leaders.

The P-40 grew out of the P-36, a Curtiss fighter of the mid-1930s. The latter airplane was a beauty to fly. The French had some in 1940, called Mohawks (Hawk 75s). The Germans wiped them out. The radial engine was replaced with the in-line Allison. Four .50cal guns replaced the .30s. With these changes, we had the P-40B.

By mid-1941, the P-40B was beefed up with six .50cal guns and armor plate, and became the P-40E.

I flew the P-40B and liked the flight characteristics. The P-40E was heavier, slower to climb, and sluggish at 20,000ft. Its radius of turn was much greater than the Japanese Zero's.

First Lieutenant Leonard Wood's fighter group was responsible for the most famous Mustang portraits ever taken. During a late-afternoon photo session from an accompanying B-17 (and not, as widely published, while returning from a mission) 361st FG commander Col. Thomas J. J. Christian leads a four-ship formation in *Lou IV*, a P-51D (44-13410, coded E2-C). The second and third P-51Ds are flown by 1st Lt. Urban L. (Ben) Drew (44-13926, coded E2-S) and Capt. Bruce Rowlett (44-13926, coded E2-A). Holding the number-four slot is a flush-canopy P-51B Capt. Francis T. Glankler 42-106811 (coded E2-H). Sadly, Colonel Christian was lost a short time after this portrait was taken. Note that only Drew's aircraft has the dorsal fillet found on late-model P-51Ds. *US Army*

Major Thomas L. Hayes, Jr., commanded the 364th FS, part of the 357th FG during the bitterly-fought first escort mission to Berlin on 6 March 1944. Hayes also fought the Japanese in Java, so he was able to compare P-39, P-40, and P-51 fighters. Here, the major is flying a P-51B model with a Malcolm hood on 8 March 1944 when a Messerschmitt Me 410 became his fifth kill and made him an ace. He was credited with 7.5 Bf 109 and one Me 410 kills, in addition to two Japanese aircraft. "Great flight characteristics," Hayes said of the Mustang. "Easy to trim and stable on instruments." He viewed it as the best fighter of the war. *Merle C. Olmsted*

The Japanese attacking Java were equipped with twin-engine Betty bombers and single-engine Zero fighters. Without early warning of attack, the air battle was usually joined with them above us. They were experienced, with five years of combat in China. Cocky and arrogant. They would barrel-roll as they commenced their dive while we were hanging by our props.

You did not turn with a Zero. It was hit and run. Deflection shooting. It should be noted, in comparison, that the AVG [American Volunteer Group] in China with their P-40Bs (later P-40Es) had a great shoot-down ratio because their early warning allowed them to get above the Japanese when the air battle began.

The Java campaign came to an end on 28 January 1942. The handwriting was clear when they cut our lifeline from Australia by their occupation of Bali on 20 February. No more P-40s. No resupply. An effort was made to bring in P-40s on the old carrier, the *Langley* (AV-3), [the Navy's first aircraft carrier, converted in 1937 to a seaplane tender with the removal of about 40 percent of its flight deck] by off-loading P-40s at the dock and taking them off on an adjacent road. However, the *Langley* was sunk by the Japanese before she could make port. I think the squadron was

Surrounding Maj. Thomas Hayes (second from left) are ground crew members S/Sgt. Bob Krull, Sgt. Gene Barsalou, and Sgt. Fred Keiper. Hayes' olive-drab P-51D fighter *Frenesi* (44-13318) bears kill markings not only for German aircraft he shot down, but for two Japanese victories as well. (Two earlier planes nicknamed *Frenesi* were a P-51B with a Malcolm canopy and a P-51C). Individual pursuit ships had their own revetments to protect them in the event of bomb damage, although at this point in the war, Luftwaffe warplanes were no longer striking airfields in England. *Merle C. Olmsted*

The 364th FS under Maj. Tommy Hayes belonged to the 357th FG, which introduced the Mustang in the Eighth Air Force. Not surprisingly, Hayes' squadron has inspired several "warbird" restorations in the 1990s. One of these is this P-51D Mustang (44-73206, registered as NL 3751D), owned by Charles Osborn and painted to represent 44-13586, *Hurry Home, Honey* flown by Capt. Richard (Pete) Peterson, one of Hayes' flight leaders. As part of the "Warbirds Over Hickory" air show held in Hickory, North Carolina, on 22 May 1994, pilot Brad Hood and back-seater Robert F. Dorr fly this 364th warbird over a rooftop of green. *Jim Sullivan*

down to its last P-40s for its final strike against the Japanese landing on the north coast. The few that returned were given to the Dutch. Evacuation was under way.

Flying personnel were flown out by air. I was in a Dutch hospital recovering from injuries in a crash landing after being shot down by a Zero. I left on a Dutch freighter along with 1,500 ground personnel and British from Malaysia to Singapore.

Back in Australia, I was assigned to the 35th Pursuit Group, being reactivated in Sydney and thence to New Guinea. We flew a British version of the P-39 that had a smaller 20mm cannon, designated the P-400. Again, we had no warning network. In 10–15 min, we usually were climbing through 8,000–9,000ft when the bombs hit, and the Japanese were streaking home to their bases on the other side of the island.

Here, the line of sight radar was blocked by the 10,000–12,000ft mountain range running down the spine of New Guinea.

Other Fighters

The P-39 was a good gun platform. The Japanese had secretly stockpiled a sizable force of single- and twin-engine aircraft in Buna. They were well camouflaged and hidden under trees. An adjacent grassy areas were used for takeoff and landing.

We made a decision to hit them. We came in under the weather. What followed demonstrated how stable the P-39 was, when we were shooting. The weather was lousy but we got under a low ceiling and rain. We caught them by surprise, made several runs, and left many burning. [Author's note: Hayes received the Silver Star for this mission]. More P-39s went back in the afternoon. The weather was better and some of the Japanese got into the air. Again, they had losses on the ground and some in the air.

It was a great airplane on the ground. Fun to taxi with that tricycle nose wheel. My dream was to taxi out the gate at Hamilton Field in northern California, get on old U.S. 99 and head for March Field some 400mi south. Holding the P-39 at 120mph, going airborne to make those 90deg turns and setting her back on the pavement. Ditto for any traffic. That would be

Major Thomas L. Hayes, Jr., commander of the 364th FS, poses in the cockpit of his P-51D Mustang, *Frenesi*, named after a popular song of the early 1940s. Early D model Mustangs, like this one, were camouflaged. Hayes' squadron belonged to the 357th FG. *via Jeffrey L. Ethell*

fun. Tooling on down the highway like that was the only thing the P-39 could do better than a P-51.

I should mention that the pilots who were assigned to the 49th FG at Darwin after Java enjoyed a great record with their P-40Es. They had good early warning with radar on islands toward Timor.

It's hard to compare the P-39 or P-40 with the P-51. It's apples and oranges. One must compare the P-51 with the 38, the 47, the 109, and the 190.

In October 1942, all pilots who'd fought the Japanese in Hawaii, the Philippines, and Java were ordered home. This move was to improve the training and manning of new units—to put some experienced guys in Training Command and move away from the blind leading the blind. Though we'd been inadequately trained and poorly equipped, and had learned the hard way, we had knowledge worth passing along. Also, I felt qualified for the big show ahead.

Back in the states I was assigned to a training unit, the 329th FG, at Hamilton Field—our squadron,

At the end of his combat tour, following 75 missions in P-51B, P-51C, and P-51D and a promotion to lieutenant colonel, 364th FS commander Thomas L. Hayes poses in his final Mustang fighter nicknamed *Frenesi* (44-13318) with crew chief S/Sgt. Robert L. Krull, assistant crew chief Sgt. Gene J. Barsalou, and armorer Sgt. Fred Keiper. Hayes' "Pilot Talk" account of Mustang flying includes personal recollections of both air-to-air and air-to-ground combat. *Brig. Gen. Thomas L. Hayes*

The father-and-son team of Jim Beasley and Jim Beasley, Jr., (Dad, in background) demonstrates a pair of beautifully restored Mustangs at the 1991 Oshkosh air show. In the foreground is the younger Jim's flying machine, thought to be P-51K 44-12852, but painted to represent P-51D 44-13318, alias *Frenesi*, the ship flown by Thomas L. Hayes, commander of the 364th FS/357th FG in World War II. The latter-day *Frenesi* is beautifully painted and cared-for, and has won many awards. *Robert S. DeGroat*

the 327th was based at what is today San Francisco's airport—with the job of transitioning new graduates from flying school into the P-39. I envied others from the Pacific who were assigned to new groups being activated.

A tragedy gave me my chance to get back into the war. The commander of the 364th FS [Capt. Varian K. White] was killed in a P-39 gunnery crash [on 20 May 1943]. I was picked to replace him. I became a squadron commander in the 357th FG.

I could sense immediately that this was a great unit. The guys were professional and dedicated. There was a strong camaraderie. Training was intense. They worked hard and they played hard.

The P-39 was a good training aircraft. Unstable and unforgiving of an error. It killed a lot of pilots. If you survived the P-39, you could fly anything. But overall, considering logistics, it was better to lose them here than overseas.

By November we completed our training. We were ready—razor sharp! After Thanksgiving on the *Queen Elizabeth*, we disembarked in Scotland and entrained to our base in England. We followed the 354th FG (Ninth Air Force) in the base-to-base movement of our training. The 354th was already flying missions in the P-51B. They were the first, the pioneer Mustang group. Our 357th was the first P-51 group in the Eighth Air Force.

We had a kind of lend-lease in reverse. The RAF had P-51s. They'd gotten 'em already equipped with Malcolm hoods. The RAF took the bird-cage canopy off and put this Malcolm job on it, and it really helped with visibility. In fact, I liked it better than the streamlined D because it bulged out behind you and you could see all around.

They bailed some of them back to us. You could still feel the outline of the British roundel under the paint where the US national insignia had been applied. [Note: other sources indicate the 357th used aircraft that were manufactured from the start for American use].

It was easy to check out in the 51 and easy to fly. The Rolls-Royce Merlin engine gave it tremendous power. And with that huge prop, one needed a strong leg to hold rudder against torque on takeoff. Great flight characteristics. Easy to trim and stable on instruments. Gave noticeable warning of a stall. Great speed and acceleration.

Only those earphones surrounding the pilot's head, and the modern-era, Cessna T-37-style parachute give us visual clues that this Mustang portrait was snapped at Oshkosh in 1991, and not over Berlin in 1944. Jim Beasley flies his P-51K Mustang, an exact replica of *Frenesi* in which Thomas L. Hayes flew many combat missions. *Robert S. DeGroat*

Fighting Potential

Most important was its range and combat radius. It could escort bombers to any target they could reach and return. Consider this. On the last mission to Schweinfurt in October 1943 (before the P-51 era) over a hundred bombers were lost *after* the shorter-legged P-47s had to leave their escort and return to base. The loss was 31 percent of those launched. The P-51 brought an end to such disasters.

Operation Argument was the effort to destroy the German Luftwaffe or, failing that, to so cripple it that the Allies would enjoy complete air superiority during the invasion. The bombers were to concentrate on the aircraft industry, aircraft assembly, engines, ball-bearing plants, etc. The German fighters had to engage the bombers. In November 1944, the American fighters were given more freedom to move afar from the bombers, to seek and pursue. The Ninth Air Force P-47s were beating up airfields. Argument

became more intense in February with increasing intensity through May.

My hat is off to the 354th group. Its P-51Bs were the Mustangs the Germans saw. They set the stage with their aggressiveness. The German pilots became fearful. When the 357th became operational in February, our goal was to be just as aggressive and capable. Don't let the Germans off the hook, we were thinking.

Aerial Victory

My second victory was on the first large-scale attack on targets in the Berlin area. Over 800 B-17s and 24s were launched. The Germans made two large fighter attacks on our aircraft. The first came between Hanover and Brunswick and met our P-47s. The second was between Magdeburg and Berlin. 357th 51s met the second attack. I was latched onto an Me 109 but lost him when distracted by a flash in my peripheral vision, then another. These were falling bombs.

I looked up. All I could see was bombers. I split-S'ed for the deck, paralleling the bombs, pulled out on the rooftops of Berlin and headed for the closest open area. I should have gotten that 109.

Later, after four of my mates rejoined, I spotted an Me 109 at low altitude. Very quickly, I closed on him—closing fast. I fired as he dropped his gear. Hey!

The crew of the 364th FS's P-51D *Frenesi* consisted of (left to right) assistant crew chief Gene Barsalou, armorer Harry Anderson, pilot Thomas L. Hayes, and crew chief Robert Krull. Anderson is appropriately draped in a belt of .50cal ammunition of the type carried by the Mustang's six, forward-firing guns. *via Jim Beasley*

He's landing, I thought, there's an airfield ahead. Instead, he crashed and burned. Poor fellow, shot down on final. I carry no guilt. He was coming in to re-service and go back up against our bombers.

Going over the Luftwaffe airfield we all got hits on twin-engine Heinkels, Ju 88s, and even some Ju 52 transports. I think it was R.C. Smith who got some nice film as he brought his nose up through the control tower, still firing. Returning to base, we shot up several locomotives and a truck convoy.

It was back to Berlin on 8 March. Today, it was an Me 410. The Germans called it a Bomber Destroyer. Loaded with rockets, large rockets, and cannons. It could do a job on our bombers when it went through them head-on. It was very effective as a night fighter. But I'll say it was a dead goose if caught by a Mustang. My only concern was my respect for the tail gunner. From dead astern, I closed gingerly and began firing from a bit beyond range at 400 to 500 yards. I had him when his right engine exploded.

[Author's note: The twin-engine Me 410, Hayes' third German kill, added to his two Japanese aerial victories, made him an ace. His eventual score was 8.5 German plus two Japanese aircraft].

I didn't like that damned P-51C model (my second plane named *Frenesi*) because the visibility was so restrictive, and it was a pain in the neck to get in and out of. Earlier, I had flown a P-51B (my first *Frenesi*) with the Malcolm canopy; it bulged out like an electric light bulb and exacted a penalty in air speed but it had better visibility to the rear. A pilot had taken my P-51B, rolled over, and dived into the ground, so I was stuck with it until we got the newer, bubble-canopy P-51Ds.

Over Munich on 16 March, it was first a quickie Me 110. "You mean I get credit for an Me 110?" [Author's note: The real designation was Bf 110]. With my overconfidence, I found myself chasing an FW 190. The pilot obliged with a lesson in how not to do it. It started at 22,000ft. He rolled over for the deck. In the dive he never flew the plane. He slipped and skidded. Power off. Almost stalling speed. Power on. When he cut the throttle, that large radial engine became one big brake. His attitude changed continuously. Even dead ahead, I led and my fire was on the side.

After the pullout, I spread my flight of four left and right. If he turned, one of us would get him. He didn't turn. He pulled away from us. Yes, it was a lesson. He made a fool out of me. I'll get the next one, I swore.

Coming back from a similar mission to Munich [on 18 March 1943, when Hayes was leading the group], we had to cross the Ruhr where the German flak was heavily concentrated. They had a lot of 88mm guns there. The German gunfire always frightened me more than German fighter aircraft did. You could see the flak. You could hear it. You could smell it, in the cockpit. This was one situation where the coolant in the Mustang's underbelly was a problem and you wished you were in P-47. It was a God-fearing situation, and I was scared to death fanned out to avoid flak. We did all sorts of aerial calisthenics to avoid taking hits but all four P-51s in my flight came home with

First Lieutenant Leonard Wood (right) of the 375th FS/361st FG poses beside a P-51C Mustang with fellow pilots Urban L. (Ben) Drew (left) and William Kemp (center). Wood arrived in England just after D-Day to begin flying Mustang missions over the continent. He was credited with two aerial victories over Luftwaffe fighters while flying the Mustang. *Leonard Wood*

Sister squadron to Leonard Wood's 375th was the 376th FS, owner of this P-51D Mustang (44-13763 coded E9-O). This Mustang lacks the dorsal fillet added on later P-51D models and wears the black and white "invasion stripes" intended to make Allied warplanes easy to recognize during the Normandy invasion. *USAF*

battle damage. After I'd landed, when they inspected the plane and I saw how much metal had hit me, I got down on knees thanking God. My crew chief, Bob Krull, said he'd do the same; he couldn't believe a P-51 could come back with so much damage.

Sure enough, a few weeks later the group intercepted a gaggle of FW 190s. I think we knocked down about 18. It was a dogfight at altitude with no dive to the deck. I claimed one 190 but my wingman said it was a 109. We argued. The combat film proved it was an Me 109. That day, the group was credited with 17 FW 190s and one Me 109. I never got another chance at a 190.

Usually, Me 109s were relatively easy. But now and then the 109 pilot put up a hell of a fight. The difference was either the pilot or the aircraft. Of course, if the pilot had over a hundred kills he knew what he was doing. Then there were considerations involving the aircraft. Did the 51 have a full fuselage tank (located behind the center of gravity)? Was the 109 low on fuel and ammo?

On this encounter, we were in a rat race at about 28,000ft. We climbed and struggled for position up to over 35,000. It was give and take. Finally, he rolled out for the deck.

"Is he low on fuel?" I wondered. We both hit compressibility at about the same time. This was not new to me. I'd experienced it several times. The airframe and its controls had reached the plane's terminal speed. The P-47, 51, and 109 are about the same, about Mach 0.77. The plane shook, stick and rudder got no response. It came out of it when you reached more dense air, around 12,000ft. We never bottomed out together. He had control before me. He rolled 180deg and pulled out. Moments later, I had control but he was gone. Out of sight.

Escort Missions

Another example of the importance of plane and pilot: A classic interception of bombers by German fighters might be 50–60 109s and 190s with a top cover of 30 Me 109s, plus or minus. Some continued for the bombers and the rest turned into the Mustangs.

In minutes, it all broke down to units of one, two pairs, and fours. There were about seven or eight as we engaged.

The ensuing fight got confused. Like an RAF pilot told me during a dogfight in the Battle of Britain, he started with another Hurricane on his wing and ended with himself on the wing of a 109. For me on this day, I was alone and there were five Me 109s. But only the leader and I were one-on-one. The other four were covering. Probably ordered to.

For what seemed an eternity (maybe 20min) it was a stand-off. Each of us struggled and jockeyed for position to close the circle. What's going on? I wondered. I knew I was just an average pilot. But, I'm thinking, unlike that German, I am in a P-51!

What's the problem? I'm wondering. Has he given up? Is he tired? Low on fuel? The game has changed, I'm thinking. His cover has joined the fight. They have coordinated their passes from different headings. They are doing all the shooting. There is a cloud cover below with tops at around 10,000ft. I do what I did on my check-out: Chopped throttle, full rudder, stick back. Snap! I'm spinning. Not flying. When I hit the overcast, I let go of the controls. The spinning stopped. I rolled my P-51 level and broke out in the clear after 15min on instruments. Back at bomber altitude I joined up with other friends and returned to base. Tomorrow will be another day, I thought.

On 16 June 1944, our 357th FG together with the 352nd FG was ordered to locate and strafe two trains between Poitiers and Angouleme, southern France. There was no information available as to position, direction, type, and contents of these trains. I called the 352nd FG and it was decided that I would arrive 10min before the 352nd at Poitiers with each of us sweeping the area south.

When the courses were drawn, it was found necessary to carry auxiliary tanks. I decided to fill the tanks and then briefed the pilots on using them as fire bombs. The 106gal tanks were far in excess of that required for the mission but were the only available tanks. On our way to the target we flew only 30min on each of the tanks, leaving them about two-thirds full with about 75gal in each tank.

As far south as the Loire River there was a solid undercast around 2,000–5,000ft. I found myself 5min early and was unable to establish radio contact with the 352nd. The only break in this cloud was the area from Poitiers to Angouleme so I proceeded to search for trains. At the marshaling yard of Poitiers, rail transportation was seen. My top cover squadron, the 363rd, heard this conversation over the R/T [radio-telephone], and when I started to let down through a haze condition, they became separated and thought I was going down to attack. I was now leading the 364th and 362nd Squadrons at 9,000ft, covering the railroad and main roads. Nothing was observed except a marshaling yard at St. Pierre, 30mi south of Poitiers, with three lines of goods cars and other stray cars totaling about 100 cars in all. About one mile north, a train of 30 goods cars was rather neatly camouflaged by being parked between a cut of trees on a sharp bend.

Rail Attack

The attack was carried out as briefed. Having two squadrons now seemed to work smoothly and not too congested.

Flying north on the sun side, I left the 362nd at 9,000ft as top cover. I made a diving turn, slipping through some cloud at 3,000ft and ended up on the

Tony is a P-51D Mustang (44-15038, coded E2-M) belonging to 1st Lt. Leonard Wood's 375th FS, a part of the 361st FG. This is a previously unpublished view of activity at the squadron's base in Little Walden, England, from which combat sorties were flown after a move from Bottisham on 28 September 1944. The squadron flew escort missions to protect bombers attacking Berlin and other targets and, as the Allies advanced, flew air-to-ground sorties as well. *Leonard Wood*

Sister squadron to Capt. Jack Ilfrey's 77th was the 79th FS/20th FG, the owner of this P-51D Mustang (44-14822) that is laying a smoke screen from under-wing containers. Ilfrey and his fellow Mustang pilots were in action long after the Allies were driving eastward on European soil, and the capability to perform low-level missions became very important. *USAF via Jack Ilfrey*

Previously unpublished shot of *Maggie*, a P-51D Mustang (44-13692) of Capt. Jack Ilfrey's 79th FS/20th FG on a combat mission over Europe in late 1944. *via Jack Ilfrey*

First Lieutenant Duane Kelso was the pilot of a P-51D Mustang (44-14365) nicknamed *Danny Boy* of the 79th FS/20th FG and is posing in front of his fighter at the group's base, King's Cliffe, England. As Capt. Jack Ilfrey's wingman on the combat mission of 20 November 1944, Kelso got to see more of German-occupied Europe than he'd bargained on, while Ilfrey discovered that the Mustang could readily be converted into a two-seater. *via Jack Ilfrey*

Previously unpublished view of Capt. Jack Ilfrey (second from right) with one of several P-51 Mustangs (44-13761) he nicknamed *Happy Jack's Go Buggy*. Originally sent to Ilfrey's family after passing the "station censor" in 1944, this snapshot shows (left to right) an unidentified ground crewman, T/Sgt. Richard Burgess, Sgt. Robert Hermes, Ilfrey, and Cpl. Roy Miller. *via Jack Ilfrey*

to a factory-fresh P-51D Mustang like the one with which he poses here. Fahey went on to join the 78th FS/15th FG and was rushed to hard-won Iwo Jima as a replacement for P-51 pilots killed in a Japanese *banzai* attack. The Mustang had an important, if little-publicized, role escorting B-29 bombers to Japan in the final months of the war. *USAF via Joe Fahey*

deck approaching the yard from the west, or 90deg to it. My flight of four was slightly staggered abreast and coming in at 400mph all firing ahead. As each one reached the cars, he released his tanks, which sprayed gasoline around. The second flight, not far behind, fired into the burst tanks, setting many of the cars afire, and then in turn released their tanks as they passed over.

My second section of eight planes at this time splashed their tanks on the 30 cars 1mi north. After setting them afire, the cars began to blow up. We all made one pass, strafing to increase damage and fire, then we pulled up to cover the 362nd while they got in on the fun. This second squadron picked out sections of cars and buildings still not burning. There was no use in strafing any more as the fires spread quickly. The Germans saw what was happening and started two flak cars to firing, one on each side of the middle train.

From above I observed several huge explosions. About every building, warehouse, and wooden goods car were burning fiercely. The ammunition train to the north was still blowing up when we left. These cars, when they exploded, burst over 1,000ft in area. Some of the cars looked like they were loaded with phosphorus bombs. There was a great deal of small caliber and heavier stuff going off for a distance of 100 yards next to the train.

So we certainly made some use of the Mustang as an air-to-ground vehicle, although its primary purpose was air-to-air. As for my final aerial victory, my last encounter was Bastille Day, 14 July 1944, over Paris. The Me 109 crashed near the Longchamps race track where races were in progress. I felt like I was celebrating Independence Day!

I named my P-51 *Frenesi*. It was a popular piece of music in the early 1940s, sung in Spanish to south of the border rhythm. It was our song, my wife and me. "Frenesi" translates, "Love me tenderly." *Frenesi* really belonged to the ground crew and they let me fly her. What an airplane! We all loved her tenderly.

I flew my first sortie on 11 February 1944 and my last on 12 August 1944, a total of 75 missions.

1st Lt. Leonard A. Wood, 375th FS/361st FG:

I was in flying class 44-A and had about 10hr in the P-40 in advanced flying school. Then I went to the RTU [replacement training unit] to get 60–80hr in P-51s.

We were supposed to land on the 5th of June [1944] at Liverpool but they told us to go out and wait awhile. So we went and cruised in the Irish Sea while the harbor was overloaded. I didn't know until the next day that the Allies were landing in Normandy.

Once we were ashore in the UK, I went to transition school at Goxhill, near the Wash. Several fighter groups had taken pilots who'd completed their combat tours and sent them to be instructors, transition pilots who came over without P-51s.

Capt. Jack Ilfrey, commander of the 79th FS/20th FG poses at King's Cliffe, England, in September 1944 with his P-51D Mustang (44-13831) nicknamed *Happy Jack's Go Buggy*. Ilfrey's remarkable decision to land in enemy territory to rescue his wingman was by no means unique, but it was courageous and it required the Mustang to perform in ways not specified in the manufacturer's brochure. *John Hudgens via Jack Ilfrey*

My first impression: the Mustang didn't have the flaw of the P-40, which didn't have enough trim control surface on it. On the P-40 you had to pull a switch to get the gear up. On the P-51 you just picked up a lever and it was there. The P-51 had enough trim tab.

In the P-51, you could turn with anything, just about. But I tried it with a Spitfire once and he could out-turn me.

Six or seven of us went to 361st FG, commanded by Col. Thomas J. J. Christian. They'd just gone through D-Day with several losses and were flying their butts off. They didn't pay a whole lot of attention to me. But they were glad to get more bodies.

I was assigned to the 375th FS. We had P-51B, C, and D models. They were mostly D. The flush-canopy Bs and Cs had a smaller profile and seemed a little faster and lighter, but the Ds offered better visibility.

I started flying missions at the end of July 1944. My first was on July 21. We went to Regensberg on bomber escort. After we turned the bomber train over to somebody else, my flight commander, Gene Cole, from Akron, Ohio, saw this airfield down below and decided to make a strafing run across it.

It was the first time I'd gone from high altitude down to the deck so fast. We started from 28,000ft. I remember seeing 550mph on the air-speed indicator. My whole cockpit fogged up. The windshield of heavy plate glass had been below freezing up there, and the sudden warming caused moisture to fog it up.

The "front office" for pilots like Iwo Jima-based Joe Fahey of the 78th FS. The cockpit of the P-51D Mustang, here seen in pristine condition, was straightforward and sensible, with mission-related switches on the center console between the pilot's knees, and rather large basic instruments such as the turn-and-bank indicator in the center of the panel. *Rockwell International*

I went across the airfield and tried to keep Cole in the little window to my left because I couldn't see a thing straight ahead! When he fired his guns, I fired my guns. I saw some of his tracers hitting the ground and bouncing up over the top of his wings. I couldn't see anything but him off to the left. The number four man in our flight didn't stay with us, and he got shot down. He should have broken off because he'd fallen too far behind. They hit him. He bailed out and became a POW.

By the time we got across the aerodrome and started pulling out, my fogged windshield started to dissipate and I could see.

I'd logged 100hr of combat by my birthday, 22 August 1944. So I got my first three-day pass to London. Until then, any libation had been limited to a medicinal shot of whiskey after each mission.

We escorted everything in those days—mostly B-24s but a lot of times B-17s. Those were the guys I admired because they just stayed right on track even when you could walk right on the flak. Once committed to a run, they stayed straight and level.

The bombers indicated 170–180mph and we indicated 230–250, so we had to do a lot of S-turns back and forth to remain in position as escorts. Flying top cover, we were 3,000–4,000ft above them. We had other fighters elsewhere going back and forth watching out for the men in those bombers.

Our tour of duty was originally 300 combat hours. This later was reduced to 275. I flew 75 missions.

I was with Captain Drew [air ace Urban L. (Ben) Drew] who'd been a P-51 instructor in the states before going overseas. We were coming back from a mission, an escort mission. For some reason we broke off going home and were shooting up a bunch of things on the deck in France. After strafing, we came right across an airfield near a well-known cathedral where a gaggle of 40 109s and 190s were taking off.

Some of those Messerschmitts and Focke-Wulfs weren't up yet. We went right on through them. They scattered in all directions. I think Drew shot one down. I think [1st Lt. William T.] Kemp hit one, and the guy bailed out. On the ground, they were crash landing and driving through fences. We were all out of ammunition because we'd been strafing.

On 2 November 1944, while escorting bombers at high altitude, we fought with a bunch who were coming at us. I shot one down. I followed him all the way down to the deck. He was a 109. At the time, I wrote:

"I was leading DECOY BLACK Flight when we encountered two Me 109s at approximately 300 feet. When we bounced them, they immediately split up. One of them started in a left orbit. Before he had completed 360 degrees, I was able to pull two rings deflection at 80 yards and observed strikes just behind the cockpit. This Me 109 immediately leveled out, glided into the ground, and exploded when it hit. I fired 876 rounds."

My wingman, 1st Lt. Caleb J. Clayton, gave a supporting statement on my Messerschmitt kill:

"I was flying DECOY BLACK Two when Lt. Wood encountered the ME-109. I observed hits to the rear of the canopy and with Lt. Wood followed the ME-109 down and saw it explode and burn." [Author's note: The quotes are from a 361st FG "encounter report." American pilots were consistent in calling the German fighter the Me 109 rather than using its correct name, Bf 109.]

About a week later, we saw some others and went diving after them. I was closing so fast, I went right on by, but my wingman, 2nd Lt. Robert J. (Bob) Farney, who was on his first mission, shot one down.

Then it was my turn. Once again, I submitted a claim in an encounter report:

"I was leading DECOY RED Flight when I saw approximately 40 FW-190s flying in three bunches of 10 to 15, at 10 o'clock and 26,000 feet. I picked out one FW-190 but overshot him. DECOY RED Two [Farney] then shot him down. I then picked out another and gave him a short burst and observed hits in and behind the cockpit. I was using the K-14 gunsight. He was less than 200 yards away and I used 15 degrees of deflection. He rolled over on his back and flew for a few seconds, then rolled out in a steep diving turn going into the ground and exploding. The pilot did not bail out. I used 181 rounds."

I was credited with two air-to-air plus damaged. After Captain Cole went home, my aircraft became 44-14085 E-2G (bar under G), named *Yvonne Marie*, and this is the plane in which my two kills were scored. My crew chief was M. Strickler.

My last Mustang flight was in about October 1952. I had joined the 172nd FS (equivalent to 375th deactivated), Michigan ANG at Kellogg Field. I joined in February 1949 and was recalled for Korea on 1 Feb 1951. I transferred to Selfridge. All of my flights were in the F-51D and I never flew the F-51H. I logged 1,157hr in the Mustang.

Capt. Jack Ilfrey, 79th FS/20th FG

We were flying mission no. 214 on 20 November 1944. 1st Lt. Duane Kelso was my wingman in my flight of P-51 Mustangs.

On this particular afternoon I led a flight of five P-51Ds to a rendezvous with two P-38 Photo Joes [designated F-5A]. We escorted and covered them while they took pictures over and around Berlin.

We were at this time in fair enough weather, 6–7/10ths overcast, and the flak had been light. When through in the Berlin area they headed southwest along the Autobahn taking more pictures along the way to Magdeburg, again picking up more intense flak. The mission then called for them to go farther in the Bonn area where our bombers had attacked airfields and synthetic oil plants earlier in the day. However, before we got there they radioed that they were going to head for home, being low on fuel and film. The fuel I could understand because they had been really barreling along in those F-5As. Also, we were now over a solid overcast with just an occasional hole here and there.

It was our habit, after escort, to hit the deck and get our kicks ground-strafing targets of opportunity on the way back home to England. By this time we were now secure in the knowledge that those P-51s made us feel like hunters in the skies over Germany. Our morale was high, during ground strafing, chasing, or evading their fighters, during dog fights, just firing the guns. We also got an adrenaline high and in my case sometimes it could reach the point of auto-eroticism also mentioned by others.

Back to the mission. We spiraled down through a hole and sure enough found plenty of trucks, tanks, and other equipment heading toward the front lines.

We were now heading in a westerly direction and at the same time sliding under a rather massive weather front.

I had been busy shooting them up and did not know exactly where we were. I told the boys to form up. Let's get together and head for home. We had expended a lot of ammunition, and our fuel supply was not in good shape. It was a little after 1600 hours. It gets dark early in that part of northern Europe. So I set course for England figuring we might have to land in Belgium or France.

Heading Home

I decided to stay below the weather front as there could still be a stream of bombers heading back through the overcast. Also I'd never forgotten, even to this day, my wandering over Hamburg in the overcast on one engine in my P-38, when that overcast turned black and red when those 88 shells vectored in real close.

We were in good formation with me still trying to get my bearings when we came right up on Maastrick, Holland, which was still in German hands, and those hands began firing at us.

I did not know it at the time, but our First and Ninth Armies had launched a massive attack in this area on 16 November 1944 east of Aachen, which had been taken on 21 October. We were headed in a north-westerly direction so I veered right, north, to get away from the city and all that ack-ack. But still we were over the middle of heavy ground action that appeared more German than American and we were picking up heavy fire. So I said, hell, we'll turn right again.

At that time my wingman, Kelso, said over the radio he had been hit and was loosing power. We were around 700–800ft in poor visibility but were getting away from the front lines. I had just seen a cleared stretch that appeared to be a small emergency-type strip surrounded by trees with a few bombed-out buildings and a few wrecked aircraft scattered around. I pointed it out and told him to try for it and that I'd attempt to cover him, knowing that we were almost out of ammo and low on fuel. I told my other three P-51 Mustang pilots that they were on their own.

They all made it okay, landing in Belgium. I said to Kelso, the strip doesn't look bad. Use your own judgment whether to try for a wheels-down landing. If you go in wheels down and think I could make it too, give me the thumbs up signal when I circle around.

In the meantime he and I both were picking up ground fire and I stayed as low to the trees as possible. He made a rather hairy wheels-down landing, stopped right near the edge of the trees, and jumped out.

A P-51D Mustang, nicknamed *Margaret IV*, on one of the three airfields on Iwo Jima, from which three P-51 groups and one P-47 group escorted bombers to the Japanese home islands. Working conditions on Iwo Jima were primitive, and the ground crews' work became more difficult when the Mustangs started flying air-to-ground missions with 5in HVAR (high velocity aircraft rockets) like those mounted beneath this P-51D. *via Joe Fahey*

I was aware that he had been fired upon while landing. I came around almost immediately, still being fired on too, and there he was with a big grin on his face, thumbs up and all.

Damn, I must have been out of my ever-loving mind. However, the thought of *not* going in never occurred to me. He was a good pilot, an excellent wingman, would have followed me anywhere, and I couldn't help but feel very close to him at this particular moment.

It flashed through my mind how Art Heiden and Jesse Carpenter had attempted this same thing [landing to rescue a downed buddy] when I was shot down earlier on June 13. I'd had a nearly fatal bailout, that time, while strafing a locomotive, and had escaped capture by the Nazis with the help of some friendly French people. Art and Jesse hadn't been able to pick me up because of the trees and glider barriers. They'd had heavy thoughts about having to leave me there deep in enemy-occupied territory.

Now, too, other flashes came through my mind of occasions in North Africa when my companions saved my life and I did likewise (94th FS, 1942–43). Friendships forged in combat are never forgotten.

Combat Landing

So, impetuously, I threw down the wheels and flaps and went in for another hairy landing. Kelso had the presence of mind to get away from his aircraft as German ground fire was still trying to hit it. He ran 100 yards or so toward the end of the strip figuring I'd turn around and take off from the way I came in, regardless of the wind, which happened to be negligible. (Lucky us.)

God, what a hairy landing, dodging holes, muddy as hell, but the *Go Buggy* made it [P-51D-5-NA 44-13761, nicknamed *Happy Jack's Go Buggy*].

Now, the adrenaline was really pumping. Taxied a short distance up to him. Set park brakes. Jumped out on the wing. Took off chute and dinghy.

He got in, sat in what was now a bucket-like seat, and lowered the seat and himself all the way. We immediately discovered that four legs were not going to fit and allow me full rudder control. So I stood up and he crossed his legs under him and I sat down on them. No time to try other positions or adjust the seat and shoulder harness.

Like to have scalped myself trying to close the canopy. Thank God it was a "D." So there I was, head and neck bent down, knees almost up to my chin.

I started a most hairy takeoff. Almost castrated myself pulling back on the stick. For a second, I thought we weren't going to make it.

Threw down some flaps, reamed out my crotch some more, and the *Go Buggy* pulled up over the trees. Thank God she was light, low on ammo and fuel.

Made a short flight to Brussels, which had been taken by the British on 3 September. Made another hairy landing—crotch bit and all.

Iwo Jima, as seen from behind a twin 40mm Bofors antiaircraft gun emplacement. This location is actually rather high above the parking apron for P-51D Mustangs, a few of which are seen in the foreground. The Mustang at front left belongs to the 72nd FS/21st FG.

The B-29 Superfortress bombers are on Iwo only because they diverted from Japan with battle damage. The unforgettable peak of Mount Surabachi, won with the blood of American marines, dominates the distant background. *via Joe Fahey*

It didn't always go well on Iwo Jima. Here, a B-29 Superfortress burns furiously after cracking up right in the middle of a flight line of P-51D Mustangs belonging to the 15th FG. *via Joe Fahey*

I've never forgotten the camaraderie I shared with Kelso over this incident. We never thought of destroying his aircraft, as we were supposed to. We were too anxious to get the hell out of there.

The next day, with no parachute or dinghy, I took the *Go Buggy* back to our 20th FG base at King's Cliffe in England. Kelso came a few days later by transport.

I guess I expected a rather rousing reception. But Colonel Rau, the group commander, was mad as hell. He said I was a squadron commander and should not have pulled a trick like that, jeopardizing myself and my aircraft. He also reminded me that I was already in hot water with Gen. Edward Anderson, commander of the 67th Fighter Wing, for damaging his P-47 earlier, and that I was on borrowed time as squadron CO. I was a captain waiting to get my majority back after having been busted to second lieutenant a couple of months earlier.

Therefore, the climax of mission no. 214 was not entered in the intelligence report.

However, it has been indelibly implanted in my mind all of these years. I have not seen or heard of Kelso since leaving the ETO in early '45.

Joe Fahey, 78th FS/15th FG

I was in flying class 44-F. Although I arrived on Iwo Jima in April [1945], I was not scheduled for missions to Japan until mid-June or so. Many of the pilots had been overseas for 24–36 months so the squadron management were trying to get their 13 missions completed so they could go home.

The *banzai* attack when ten P-51 pilots were killed was probably the second or third week in March 1945, while I was en route. They were Mustang pilots with the 72nd FS/21st FG. The Japanese attacked wearing Marine uniforms, at night; they opened the slit tents and threw grenades in. At the time of this sudden loss of life among Mustang pilots, I was in Honolulu preparing to travel by sea to Iwo Jima. I was one of ten Mustang pilots chosen to fly, instead, on a Consolidated F-7 Liberator, a photo-reconnaissance version of the B-24 pressed into service as a "rush" transport. We flew by way of Johnson Island, Kwajelein, and Guam. We arrived at Iwo on the day before the first big fighter strike and went straight into a briefing.

There were three airstrips on Iwo Jima and all were used to put up that mission, where the Mustangs took off and circled over the island, 48 planes on the strike with two spares.

I quickly got used to the life of a Mustang pilot on Iwo.

Upon arrival on Iwo, the 78th enlisted men and officers (who followed my group of ten pilots by sea) slept in fox holes at night. The Marines and Army were still fighting at the north end of Iwo in April '45.

When the fog was bad, and sometimes you could not see across the runway, Radar would notify stranded B-29 crews when to jump out (over the island). The pilot/co-pilot would put the B-29 on autopilot and bail out on the second pass over the island. If a P-61 was over the island, he could then shoot down the B-29. One of those P-61 pilots was interviewed on the armed services radio network. We had planes go out on secret missions in the middle of the night to try to shoot down high ranking Japanese officials. Destroyers and radar picket ships were part of this team. We never were successful.

Night or day, the ground crew had work to do. This mechanic on a metal stanchion is working on the cowling of a P-51D Mustang of the 15th FG on Iwo Jima. *via Joe Fahey*

P-51D Mustang 44-63299 of the 78th FS/15th FG carries out a "stores separation" test with a factory-made wing tank. *via Joe Fahey*

There was also a mission in which we lost 27 P-51s and 26 pilots, with one guy being rescued by a submarine. When a pilot got shot down twice, he was rotated back to the states. For air-sea rescue, we had a helicopter, a large Sikorsky, and at least one B-17 with a raft attached to it. [Note: Other sources indicate that the Sikorsky R-4, the only helicopter in use at the time, did not reach Iwo Jima].

We were told not to tell the Japanese top secret plans or about radar if we were captured, and if they started to torture or physically hurt us, we were told not to lie to them. Supposedly, Tokyo Rose knew the names of some of our squadron commanders, like Lieutenant Colonel Crimm, the CO of the white-nosed Mustangs (76th FS/21st FG).

Occasionally a Japanese Betty would be shot down over Iwo.

We had a lot of engine failures on takeoff due to the volcanic dust fouling spark plugs. This was eliminated when they removed the steel mat runway and replaced it with asphalt.

One problem: black sand beach. They laid adobe or something over it. When you took off, you created a dust storm. A lot of engine failures on takeoff, usually fatal. Seabees paved runways. Why an engine failure on takeoff fatal? The most dangerous part of flying. No place to go except the ocean. Mustang doesn't ditch. That scoop underneath you does an outside loop in the water. 8 inches in front of face is gunsight. A guy who ditched, with straps tight may have pulled 30, 40, 50g, pulled the straps, busted helmet, hit gunsight, but survived.

Air Battle

Bounced by Japs one day. Told to drop wing tanks. Forgot to switch fuel tanks. Was doing 450mph. Lost control but regained it, fired up, and went on my way. Eventually learned to think rationally rather in a state of panic.

A number of our pilots did very well in air-to-air action with what remained of the waning Japanese air arm, and we produced at least one ace. I know of no one in our fighter group who would have traded the P-51D Mustang for any other airplane. We often had difficult circumstances to deal with, but we knew when flying the enemy that we had an excellent chance of facing all the dangers, facing the Japanese, and getting back alive to talk about it later.

CHAPTER 4

Foreign Mustangs

The Mustang is perhaps the only well-known American fighter that owes its origins to another country. Had it not been for Great Britain, the P-51 would never have been.

No full exposition of the countries that operated Mustangs has previously been published. The following account has a few obvious gaps but is intended as a *tour d'horizon* of the Mustang overseas. Some of the details that follow are published here for the first time.

Australia

Before Australia operated its own Mustangs, Australian pilots pressed the hard-fought European war as members of RAF Mustang squadrons. One of these men, Flying Officer John Haslope, shot down an Me 163 rocket-powered fighter while flying a Mustang Mk III with the RAF's No. 165 Squadron on 10 April 1945.

Beginning in November 1944 at the backwater of Fano, Italy, the Royal Australian Air Force's (RAAF) No. 3 Squadron, began to receive Mustang Mk III and Mk IV (P-51B/C and P-51D/K) fighters. The Mustangs arrived as replacements for the proven but weary Kittyhawk, a version of the P-40. All had originally been ordered for British use and retained RAF serials. The Australians used their new planes to support partisan operations in Yugoslavia. The squadron was also credited with destroying vital bridges, marshaling yards, and other targets in the final months of the European war.

Beginning in 1945, Australia took delivery of its first American-built P-51D Mustang (A68-1001) intended to serve as a "pattern aircraft" for subsequent American- and Australian-built airplanes. This aircraft was followed by Lend-Lease deliveries of 215 P-51D (A68-1001; A68-600/813) and 84 P-51K (A68-500/583) Mustangs from the United States. First to take on the Mustangs were the RAAF's Nos. 84 and 86 Squadrons at Townsville, Queensland. At the time, it was expected that these squadrons would fight in

the expected amphibious invasion to defeat the Japanese on their home soil. They were preparing for the final fight at Labuan, North Borneo, when the war ended. Both squadrons were disbanded shortly after Japan's surrender.

During the occupation of Japan, Australia was a participant in what became known as the British Commonwealth Air Force (BCAIR). This tri-national air arm included two British Spitfire squadrons, a New Zealand Corsair squadron, and the RAAF's No. 81 Wing, uprooted from Labuan, Borneo, and consisting of the Mustang-equipped Nos. 76, 77, and 82 Squadrons. Number 81 Wing took up its occupation stations at Iwakuni and Bofu, Japan, in the spring of 1946. Numbers 76 and 82 Squadrons remained until 1949 when they were withdrawn to Australia. Of these six squadrons of propeller-driven British Commonwealth fighters, only one, No. 77 Squadron, was available (at Iwakuni) when the Korean War began on 25 June 1950.

Plans were well advanced to withdraw No. 77 Squadron when the North Koreans invaded across the 38th Parallel. Operating first from Iwakuni, Japan, and later from Pohang, Korea, the RAAF Mustang squadron did some very hard fighting that saw the loss of squadron commander, Wing Commander Lou Spence, to North Korean ground fire on 3 September 1950. His successor as commander was Squadron Leader Richard Creswell, who had previously commanded No. 77 in 1942 when it was flying Kittyhawks against the Japanese.

After the Chinese intervened in November 1950, No. 77 Squadron was temporarily moved to Yonpo in

The RAAF's No. 23 Squadron shows off its CA-18 Mustangs at RAAF Richmond in the 1950s. Also visible in this shot are Wirraway trainers, a Lincoln bomber, and C-47 transports. The aircraft in the foreground (A68-135) was manufactured by Commonwealth and delivered to the RAAF in December 1948. Australia operated both home-built and NAA-manufactured Mustangs in the 1940s and 1950s. *Ron Purssey via Bruce Potts*

North Korea. Later, No. 77 was withdrawn to Pusan. The last Australian combat mission in a Mustang was flown on 6 April 1951 after which the squadron converted to the Gloster Meteor Mk VIII. In 3,800 Mustang sorties during the Korean War, No. 77 Squadron lost 18 airplanes and eight pilots.

While World War II was still being fought, the RAAF chose the P-51D Mustang for license production to meet its need for a long-range fighter to operate in the Southwest Pacific. Australia acquired a complete aircraft and 100 assembly kits, 80 of which (A68-1/80) were assembled by Commonwealth as the CA-17 Mustang Mk XX, or Mustang Mk 20. Powered by the Packard V-1650-3 Merlin engine, the first aircraft in this series flew on 29 April 1945 and was turned over to the RAAF on 4 June 1945.

Soon afterward, Commonwealth manufactured 14 Mustang Mk XXII, or Mustang Mk 22 reconnais-sance aircraft (A68-81/94) with F24 oblique cameras, distinguished by a camera port on the left rear fuselage. These photo ships were delivered between July and December 1947.

The manufacturer also delivered 40 CA-18 Mustang Mk XXIs, or Mustang Mk 21s in two batches (A68-95/120; A68-187/200) powered by the V-1650-7 engine, and 66 Mustang Mk XXIIIs, or Mustang Mk 23s (68-121/186) with British-built Rolls-Royce Merlin 70 engines. The Merlin 70 was a development of the "60 series" first proposed for Australian Mustangs in July 1945 and equipped with revisions to the supercharger unit. This version of the famous Merlin engine was first flown in Australia aboard a P-51D Mustang (A68-1001) earlier used as a "pattern aircraft" for the Mustang program; this aircraft formerly belonged to the USAAF (as 44-13293) and was used in developmental work in Australia for many years.

The outfit is No. 23 Squadron at Archerfield, and the key word is trouble. Something went seriously wrong when, attempting a fast exit, the Australian wing leader inadvertently crossed the path of wingman Ron Purssey's CA-18 Mustang (foreground), causing the two fighters to chew each other up with their propellers. A68-163, Purssey's plane in foreground, was built by Commonwealth and delivered to the RAAF in October 1949. The markings shown are typical of those employed by the RAAF in the early 1950s. *Ron Purssey via Bruce Potts*

An Australian Wirraway, distant relative of the NAA trainers, leads the way for a Mustang fighter on a routine flight in the early 1950s. The aircraft in the background is A68-138, a Commonwealth-built CA-18 Mustang Mark 23 delivered to the RAAF in January 1949.
Bruce Potts

An Australian pilot warms up and prepares to take off. A68-527 is a NAA-built P-51K Mustang (44-12605) belonging to the RAAF's No. 84 Squadron at Ross River, Townsville, in the mid-1940s. This ship was delivered to the Australian air arm in April 1945, and was struck off charge in December 1948. *Ken Hutchison via John Hunt*

Although not of top quality, this aerial portrait is as rare as they get—a shot of the Commonwealth CA-15 on an early test flight over Australia. The CA-15 strongly resembled the Mustang and grew from similar long-range-mission requirements. Too late for service in the Second World War, the CA-15 first flew on 4 March 1946 and was tested for four years before being scrapped. *John Hunt*

The total of 120 CA-18 Mustangs (in Mks 21, 22, 23) was a drop from early plans for production of 170 of this version. The designation CA-21 was applied to further planned aircraft that were canceled before construction began.

The CA-18 aircraft had minor modifications as compared with earlier Australian-built ships. They had 10in (254mm) diameter disc brakes fitted instead of 7in (178mm) units, a molded laminated wooden pilot's seat in place of the earlier magnesium alloy sheet and tube seat, and minor changes to the engine warning light and gunsight.

Adding CA-17 and CA-18 production, the total number of Mustangs produced in Australia was 200, rather than the 690 that had once been foreseen. The RAAF for a long time had more fighters than it needed, and the 200th indigenous Mustang was not delivered until April 1951, five years after the first. The RAAF acquired 214 P-51Ds and 84 P-51Ks from USAAF inventory.

Commonwealth also built and flew its own design, the CA-15, which strongly resembled the Mustang and also grew from long-range mission requirements. Too late for service in the war, the CA-15 flew on 4 March 1946 and was tested for four years before being scrapped.

Among many ex-RAAF Mustangs found on Australia's civil registry was a CA-18 Mustang Mk 23 (A68-187) that was purchased in 1969 by Sydney

FAB 520 is a Cavalier F-51D Mustang (67-22580), manufactured on 24 November 1967 and turned over to the Bolivian Air Force on 19 January 1968. The slender, tall vertical fin on an aircraft that is otherwise clearly a D model is the mark of the Cavalier conversions. Bolivia eventually traded its Mustangs in on Canadair T-33s, after which this Mustang became a civilian, wearing registry C-GXUR. It's seen at Great Falls, Montana, apparently on its return from Bolivia, on 23 December 1977. Note the hasty application of the Canadian registry number on the tail and the graffiti elsewhere on the aircraft. *Arnold Swanberg*

businessman Hockey Treloar with the intention of converting the aircraft to use a Rolls-Royce Dart turboprop engine. A similar conversion was made in the United States at about the same time (chapter one). This turboprop conversion never proved successful and this "warbird," civil-registered as VH-UFO, was eventually restored to Merlin power.

Bolivia

Bolivia, a landlocked South American republic with mountainous terrain, operates the Fuerza Aerea Boliviana or FAB, a modest air arm that in the 1970s became one of the very last users of the Mustang.

For more than a decade, Bolivian military aviation limped along with several aircraft types but without a sufficient number of any type to be effective. During July 1954, the FAB acquired three Mustangs (two F-51Ds and a TF-51D). The following month, four Bolivian pilots trained with the 182nd FS, Texas ANG, at Brooks Field near San Antonio. This squadron was flying Mustangs although they were F-51H models.

In 1967, Trans-Florida (re-named Cavalier that same year) received a USAF contract for "new build" F-51D Mustangs to be delivered to several Latin countries. Over time, nine of the remanufactured Cavalier Mustangs, six F-51Ds, and three TF-51Ds, were added to Bolivia's order of battle. They joined a Mustang force that eventually included 16 NAA-built fighters for a total of 25 aircraft. No fewer than five Mustangs, or 20 percent of the force, were lost in mishaps.

Some ex-Bolivian Mustangs have now found their way to the US civil register as part of the burgeoning warbird community in the United States.

Canadian pilots flew two generations of Mustangs. World War II veterans served with Nos. 400, 414, 420, 430, 441, and 442 Squadrons flying various models of the P-51 from early in the conflict until V-J Day. In 1945, the RCAF picked up 100 surplus P-51D Mustangs, like the Canadian Warplane Heritage's ship no. 9567 shown at Trenton on 11 September 1982, and flew them until 1956. They equipped both regular and auxiliary fighter squadrons and training units. *via Dan Hagedorn*

FAB 522 is a two-seat Cavalier TF-51D Mustang wearing shark's teeth and the livery of the Bolivian Air Force, or Fuerza Aerea Boliviana. Nine remanufactured Cavalier fighters, including six F-51Ds and three TF-51Ds, were operated in Bolivia together with 16 NAA-built aircraft. One of the very last operational users of the Mustang, Bolivia experienced its share of mishaps with the aircraft and eventually removed them from service. *via Dan Hagedorn*

When the US armed forces occupied the Dominican Republic in 1965, they captured FAD 1919, one of the P-51D Mustangs operated by that country's air force. The Cuerpo de Aviacion Militar purchased 44 F-51D Mustangs (FAD 1900/1943) from Sweden in October 1952. In the 1950s, the Dominican air arm had two fighter squadrons, one with F-51D Mustangs and the other with F-47D Thunderbolts and Vampires F.Mk Is. Plans to replace the propeller-driven fighters with new F-86F Sabres never materialized. *USAF*

Canada

Canadian pilots flew Mustangs during World War II. Throughout the British Commonwealth, member nations expanded their own air forces and also formed squadrons to serve alongside British RAF units and under RAF command. Royal Canadian Air Force (RCAF) squadrons in the RAF were numbered from 400 to 443. Among these were Canada's Mustang units:

• No. 400 Squadron formed at Odiham in 1941 and went from Lysanders to Tomahawks to Mustang Mk Is. After risky tactical reconnaissance missions over occupied Europe in 1943–44, the squadron con-

verted to Mosquito and Spitfire photo-reconnaissance planes in mid-1944.

• No. 414 Squadron went from Tomahawks to Mustang Mk Is and flew the Mustangs at Dieppe in August 1942 on tactical reconnaissance missions in support of the Canadian landings. Operating from Croydon, the squadron then flew offensive operations and shipping reconnaissance over the French coast. In 1943, the squadron made a number of moves to various airfields in England and in mid-1944 flew tactical reconnaissance leading up to D-Day. The squadron re-equipped with Spitfire Mk IXs before moving to the continent after the Normandy invasion.

• No. 420 Squadron operated as a bomber unit during the war (Hamden, Halifax, Lancaster) but became a postwar operator of P-51D Mustangs when disbanded as an RAF unit and was re-established at home after the war.

• No. 430 Squadron was the third Canadian squadron assigned to the "army co-operation" mission, initially with Curtiss Tomahawks but in due course with early Mustang Mk Is. This squadron flew

The Dominican Republic was one of the best-known, and one of the last, users of the NAA P-51 Mustang. In addition to 44 former Swedish Mustangs, the Cuerpo de Aviacion Militar operated at least one F-6K photo ship. The shark-toothed Mustang seen here on the flight line in 1974 wears the serial FAD 1900, which apparently was applied to two different aircraft. The camouflage paint scheme on Dominican Mustangs was applied with great care. *Vincent Tirado via Dan Hagedorn*

offensive missions over Nazi-occupied Europe, shifted to a defensive role for a period in 1943, then became involved in preparations for the Normandy offensive. For a time after D-Day, the squadron escorted Hawker Typhoon fighter-bomber elements to photograph their results. After the invasion, the squadron flew hundreds of road and transport reconnaissance missions. No. 430 went ashore in Europe and began leapfrogging eastward, operating from various bases, before giving up its Mustangs for Spitfire Mk XIVs in November 1944.

• No. 441 Squadron was in the process of completing a conversion from Spitfire Mk IXs to Mustang Mk IIIs when the war ended.

• No. 442 Squadron converted from Spitfires to Mustang Mk IVs on 23 March 1945.

In 1945, the RCAF purchased 100 former USAAF P-51D Mustangs. Until declared obsolete at the end of 1956, these equipped both regular and auxiliary fighter squadrons and training units.

China

China received P-51D Mustangs directly from the US before the end of World War II. These were used by the Nationalist air arm in the 1946–49 civil war against the communists. A few may also have been operated by the communist side. A significant number of F-51D Mustangs reached Taiwan in 1949 and, as late as the mid-1950s one of the Chinese Nationalist Air Force's five fighter wings was equipped with F-51Ds and RF-51Ds.

Cuba

Cuba received some F-51Ds in 1947 as military assistance from the United States under the Rio Pact. These were in service with the Cuban Military Air Force, or Fuerza Aerea Ejercito de Cuba (as the country's former Aviation Corps, or Cuerpo de Aviacion, was re-named in a 1955 reorganization) until replaced with Soviet equipment in 1960. The Batista air force used some P-51s against Fidel Castro's revolutionary forces in 1959.

Dominican Republic

During the long reign (1930–61) of the authoritarian Rafael Trujillo, the Dominican Military Aviation Corps became the first Latin American user of the Mustang. The earliest Dominican Mustangs were a mixed bag of half a dozen P-51A, P-51C, and P-51D fighters (nos. FAD 1700/1705) all acquired in 1948. The Cuerpo de Aviacion Militar subsequently purchased 44 F-51D Mustangs (FAD 1900/1943) from Sweden, along with a batch of Vampire F. Mk Is, in October 1952. To confuse matters, at least one more Mustang was obtained elsewhere since research by John Dienst and Dan Hagedorn shows that two planes wore number FAD 1900, one a former Swedish ship and the other an F-6K reconnaissance craft.

In the mid-1950s, the Dominican air arm had two fighter squadrons, one equipped solely with F-51D Mustangs and the other operating both F-47D Thunderbolts and Vampires. Plans to replace the propeller-driven fighters with new F-86F Sabres never materialized.

After setting some kind of a longevity record, the last twelve aircraft were still operating from Santo Domingo in 1984, when they were retired and sold off to private owners, the last operational Mustangs in the world.

France

A few former USAAF P-51 and F-6 Mustangs came into the hands of France's Armee de l'Air shortly after V-J Day.

Great Britain

The British search for fighters in the early days of the Second World War led to the design, development, and production of the Mustang. Employment of the Mustang by the RAF is interwoven throughout the narrative, which appears in other chapters of this volume.

An overhead look at an early Mustang Mark I for Great Britain provides a feeling for fuselage, wing, and tail shape, and for the perch occupied in the flush-canopy model by its pilot. The air scoop atop the fuselage is associated with the Allison liquid-cooled engine found on early models. The three-blade propeller was soon replaced by a four-blade model. *Rockwell*

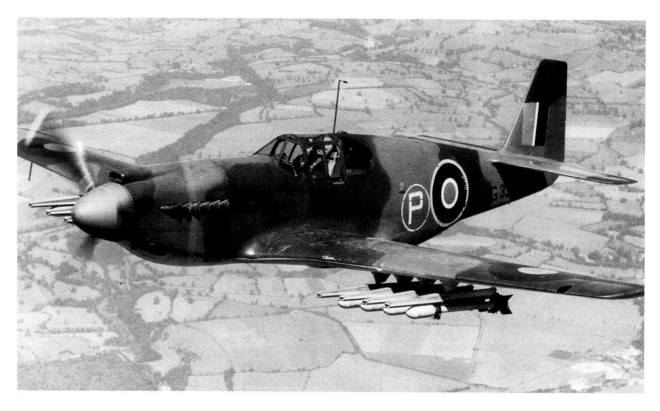

The encircled P is a British Commonwealth marking for a prototype. AG357 is the 13th Mustang Mark I manufactured by NAA for the RAF and is carrying a typical load of rocket projectiles. Great Britain later employed bubble-canopy versions of the Mustang. In British service, however, the long-range Mustang never drew the loyal following enjoyed by the shorter-range Supermarine Spitfire, which was produced in larger numbers. *RAF*

Guatemala

The Fuerza Aerea Guatemalteca, or Guatemalan Air Force, acquired its first three F-51D Mustangs on 27 July 1954, making it the first Central American operator of the type. The first three ships were delivered to Castillo forces, then seeking to take over the country from the Arbenz government, which was viewed by the United States as communist. When Castillo came to power, a second batch of three F-51D Mustangs was supplied by the United States, reaching Guatemala on 20 December 1954.

Other Mustangs followed, many of them formerly Canadian, and at least one was a two-seat TF-51D. The final tally was 30 Mustangs in service in the Guatemalan Air Force, where the planes occupied portions of four composite squadrons. The Mustangs remained in service until the early 1970s.

Haiti

The Haitian Air Corps, or Corps d'Aviation, a branch of the Garde d'Haiti, received six F-51D Mustangs in the immediate postwar years. These Mustangs formed part of a composite squadron at Bowen Field, Port-au-Prince, and were used for internal policing. The last aircraft was retired in 1975.

Honduras

Honduras used a small number of F-51Ds until 1959 when they were replaced by ten refurbished F4U-5 Corsairs pending the arrival of jet equipment.

Indonesia

When Indonesia became independent on 27 December 1949, its air arm (AURI—Angkatan Udara Republik Indonesia) was slated to receive two squadrons of F-51D Mustangs from the departing Netherlands air arm. On 21 June 1950, the Nertherlands Indies Air Force was disbanded and its airfields and aircraft were turned over to the Dutch, including F-51Ds that equipped No. 1 Squadron. By 1955, this was part of a Composite Air Group equipped with Mustangs, B-25 Mitchells, C-47s, and other types.

The AURI used F-51D and F-51K Mustangs in several internal conflicts in the postwar years.

Israel

Israel, founded on 14 May 1948, has relied heavily on its Israeli Defense Force/Air Force (IDF/AF) in crisis after crisis with neighboring Arab countries.

During 1948–49, a handful of airmen fought for Israel's independence using a hodgepodge mix of airplanes, among them Messerschmitt Bf 109s and Spitfire LF.Mk9s. Most of the aircraft and flight training for Israeli and foreign pilots waging this battle for independence came from Czechoslovakia. After

This F-51D Mustang at La Aurora airfield in Guatemala looks much too pristine to be anything but a display specimen, like the bombs and rockets that hang under its wings. In fact, the aircraft is almost certainly FAG 336, which previously was displayed in front of an apartment building in the capital. Guatemala flew a mix of Mus- tangs, some of which had served previously in Sweden and Canada and some of which were cannibalized from parts of several aircraft. At one time, Guatemala had an aerobatics team that used T-6s, T-33s, and F-51s. *Guatemalan Air Force*

FAG 336 is a NAA F-51D Mustang acquired by the Guatemalan Air Force in March 1956 and used operationally before being placed on display (as shown here) in somewhat ratty condition in front of an apartment building in Guatemala City. The former USAF serial num- bers of most Guatemalan Mustangs remain unknown and some of them met no more noble disposition than to be scrapped for their metal. *Guido E. Buehlmann*

Often, the survival of a photograph may result from the work of several. In this example, photographer Harold G. Martin's camera work was saved by Robert J. Pickett and, after both men died, was made available by Dan Hagedorn. Martin was fortunate enough to be in Miami on a bright day in the 1950s when he spotted aircraft 15655, an F-51D Mustang operated by the Haitian Army Corps. Few photos were ever taken of Haiti's half-dozen Mustangs and this one is taxiing away fast. *Harold G. Martin*

fighting had begun, the fledgling IDF/AF designated its fighter outfit as No. 101 Squadron and received just two P-51D Mustangs. First combat was flown by Gideon Lichtman, an American flying with the IDF/AF who had previously flown P-51s in the Pacific.

The first combat was anticlimactic. In October 1948, pilot Lichtman flew a reconnaissance mission to Beirut and Damascus. Near the end of the mission, Lichtman was attacked by an Arab fighter that may

In the only known photo of the sole P-51D Mustang employed by Israel's fledgling air arm in the 1948 conflict, pilot Gideon Lichtman prepares to strap into the cockpit for a mission. The Mustang is coded D-141, though the number is not visible here. Lichtman was more successful in claiming aerial victories against Israel's neighbors while flying a Messerschmitt Bf 109. *via Brian Cull*

Wearing the gold and black checkerboard markings of No. 4 (Otago) Squadron of the TAF is NAA F-51D-30-NT Mustang NZ2406/45-11495. Single-point refueling was still by no means a standard in aviation, and this ground crew member is working hard to fill the Mustang with gas. *RNZAF*

have been a Hawker Sea Fury. When he sought to engage, his guns jammed. The Mustang pilot came home without having fired a shot.

The pair of Mustangs belonging to the fledgling IDF/AF flew several dozen combat missions and toted up at least one aerial kill before the 1948–49 war ended.

In September 1952, Israel reached an agreement with Sweden to take delivery of 25 F-51D Mustangs for service in the IDF/AF. The Mustangs arrived between November 1952 and June 1953 and were pressed into duty with the IDF/AF's No. 102 Squadron.

IDF/AF F-51D Mustangs saw plenty of action during the Suez Crisis fighting that began with Israel's attack on Egypt on 29 October 1956. Two Mustangs were assigned to cut Egyptian phone lines using special hooks trailing from long cables: when these devices failed to work, the Mustang pilots did the job with their wing leading edges and sustained only minor dents.

Mustangs were quietly retired from Israeli service and a few have been salvaged as warbirds.

Italy

The Italian Air Force operated 48 F-51D Mustangs between 1948 and 1953.

Korea

When the Republic of Korea, or ROK, was established on 15 August 1948 south of the 38th Parallel, its first military aircraft were L-4 Cub and T-6 Texan trainers. When the Korean War began with the North Korean invasion of the south on 25 June 1950, Korean pilots with wartime operational experience were given conversion courses in Japan on the F-51D Mustang. These men formed the first operational squadron of the ROK Air Force (ROKAF), or Taehan Minguk Konggun, commanded by Col. Kim Shin, who had fought in China with General Chennault's American Volunteer Group, the "Flying Tigers."

The South Korean Mustangs were initially used for defensive purposes, but in the autumn of 1952, the first ROKAF wing was formed with additional Mustangs and began flying close support missions.

Netherlands

Before V-J Day, the Netherlands received 40 P-51Ds for use by the Netherlands East Indies Air Force. In the East Indies, there was a strong nationalist movement that made itself felt in sporadic fighting between Netherlanders and Indonesians. Here, the Netherlands Army Air Corps was operating three

Out of the closet after a protracted hibernation, this silvery F-51D-30-NT Mustang (NZ2406/45-11495) was the first to fly in New Zealand. Purchased while the Second World War was unresolved, thirty of these ships arrived only after V-J Day when they were no longer needed and went into storage. Many years later, this Mustang lifted off from Ardmore for delivery to RNZAF base Wigram on 19 August 1951. That flight was made by Squadron Leader R. F. Fuller, who was not even a New Zealander but an RAF exchange officer. *RNZAF Official G1365*

New Zealand's Mustangs never had a chance to fight for their country (Corsairs did, and a squadron of Corsairs had a pivotal role in the postwar occupation of Japan), but when they finally emerged from half a decade in mothballs, these ships performed yeoman service with the TAF. In the foreground, rocket-armed F-51D-30-NT Mustang (NZ2418/45-11508) warms up, part of a row of fighters preparing to go upstairs during camp at RNZAF Base Ohakea on 25 February 1954. By this time, the Mustang era "down under" was nearing its end. Presentation of the USAF serial on the tail of the ship in foreground was unusual in New Zealand service. *RNZAF Official G2567*

One of the first NAA F-51D Mustangs delivered to South Korea in the "Bout One" project in mid-1950, ship No. 3 is seen in full ROKAF (Republic of Korea Air Force) markings, but many early combat missions in the 1950-53 conflict were made possible by American pilots. This portrait was apparently snapped at Taegu air base, also known as K-2, where pilots had to cope with more dirt than concrete. *Duane E. Biteman*

fighter squadrons, No. 120 with Curtiss P-40N Warhawks and Nos. 121 and 122 Squadrons with P-51D Mustangs. The Mustangs flew in combat frequently during the upheaval that, only belatedly, led to the formation of Indonesia on 21 December 1949.

New Zealand

While the Allies were deciding how to defeat and occupy Japan, 1945 negotiations between US and New Zealand officials led to a decision by the Royal New Zealand Air Force (RNZAF) to acquire 370 Mustangs. These were expected to complement the RNZAF's Vought F4U Corsairs in the final battle against Japan and replace them after the war. The first batch was to consist of 30 P-51D-25-NT aircraft. The remaining 137 of an initial batch of 167 fighters (to be followed later by 203 more) were scheduled to be P-51M lightweight fighters.

The end of the war in the Pacific made a 370-plane Mustang purchase superfluous to New Zealand's needs. But the first 30 aircraft were already en route. The purchase of these could not be canceled.

These 30 P-51D-25-NT Mustangs built by NAA in Dallas (45-11490/11496; 45-11498/11513; 45-11515/11519; 45-11521/11522, which became NZ2401/2430) were delivered to the RNZAF in 1945 but not introduced into service. The Mustangs were stored and no decision about them was made until New Zealand decided to breathe new life into its Territorial Air Force (TAF), a Reserve component that had operated flying squadrons in the past and was revived after the war. The TAF's No. 4 Squadron received the first four Mustangs to be finally placed into flying status in late 1951. The first aircraft to fly (NZ2406) flew from storage in Ardmore to RNZAF base Wigram on 19 August 1951, piloted by Squadron Leader R. F. Fuller, an RAF exchange officer.

The TAF's four squadrons (Nos. 1, 2, 3, and 4) operated the 30 Mustangs but suffered mishaps that destroyed ten of them, or one-third of the force, by 1955. Mustangs remained in service with TAF squadrons until August 1955 when, due to mounting problems of landing gear weakness and coolant system corrosion, all were withdrawn from service.

South Africa's No. 2 Cheetah Squadron flew F-51D Mustangs like ship number 335 as a part of the USAF's 18th FBG in Korea. The South Africans suffered very high casualties and lost an enormous number of aircraft in combat, testimony to the difficulty of flying low-level missions in a fighter with a vulnerable, under-fuselage coolant unit. Like all South African F-51Ds, ship number 335 was on loan from the USAF as it taxied at K-10 Chinhae airfield during combat operations in 1951. Pretoria's intrepid fliers never had Mustangs back home. *Pancho Pasqualicchio*

Four Mustangs had a brief, second life in a drogue towing role until being retired in 1957.

Three former RNZAF Mustangs later flew as civilian warbirds. One of these (NZ2415/45-11505, registered as ZK-TAF) is currently due to return to flying status together with a recently imported F-51D warbird (44-73420), which never served in the RNZAF. The latter aircraft was expected to be restored in the olive green paint scheme of New Zealander Flt. Lt. Jack Cleland who served with the USAAF's 363rd FS/357th FG in mid-1944.

Nicaragua

The Fuerza Aerea de Nicaragua equipped one fighter squadron with 26 former Swedish F-51Ds in 1954, operating alongside a fighter-bomber squadron equipped with F-47D Thunderbolts. Both of the well-known World War II fighters were used until 1964.

Philippines

The Philippine Republic was inaugurated on 4 July 1946 and its Army Air Corps was renamed the Philippine Air Force on 3 July 1947, although it did not become an independent service branch until 23 December 1950. From its inception as a state, the Philippines was embroiled in conflict with its Huk-balahap guerrillas. F-51D Mustangs, together with C-47 transports, were employed in the campaign against the Huks. By the mid-1950s, the Philippines began disposing of its small force of F-51D Mustangs, and these were dispersed to various other countries.

South Africa

The South African Air Force (SAAF) committed its No. 2 "Cheetah" Squadron to the United Nations (UN) effort in the Korean War. Although the SAAF never flew Mustangs at home, the Flying Cheetahs flew F-51D Mustangs as a part of the USAF's 18th Fighter-Bomber Wing (FBW) beginning in late 1950.

Korean operations began on 16 November 1950 when five Mustangs began missions from K-9 airfield near Pusan, Korea, on 19 November 1950. At this juncture, the allies occupied most of North Korea and the Cheetah soon moved to K-24 airfield at Pyongyang. China's entry into the Korean War reversed the allies' fortune and No. 2 Squadron, with its parent wing, withdrew to K-13 airfield at Suwon

Mustangs reached Sweden first at the hands of USAAF pilots seeking refuge during World War II, and later from a direct purchase. The Mustang was designated J26 in Swedish service and many, like this one, were flown by F16 wing. One hundred sixty-one Mustangs served in Sweden, assigned *Flygvapen* serial numbers 26001/26161, and 12 of them later became S26 photo-reconnaissance aircraft. This ship is ready to be exhibited at the Swedish Air Force museum at Malmen on 20 May 1989. *Lars Olausson*

and then K-10 airfield at Chinhae at the southernmost tip of Korea. This remained the permanent home base for the Cheetah but air-to-ground missions were flown from forward locations at K-9, K-16 airfield at Seoul, and K-46 airfield at Hoengsong.

It was a dirty, low-level war for Mustang pilots in Korea, who were given the close-support mission and expected to strike enemy targets with rockets, napalm, and conventional bombs despite exceedingly heavy ground fire. Two SAAF Mustangs were shot down by MiG-15s, but the painful magnitude of the "Cheetahs'" casualties can be understood only when we remember that of the 95 Mustangs loaned to

No. 2 Squadron, 74 were lost in combat or in non-combat mishaps. The SAAF's Mustangs flew 10,373 sorties in Korea with 12 pilots killed in action, 30 missing or captured, and four wounded. The Mustang story ended on 31 December 1952 when the Cheetah stood down temporarily before re-equipping with F-86F Sabres.

Sweden

The Kungliga Svensk Flygvapen or Royal Swedish Air Force (which subsequently dropped the "Royal" modifier from its name in 1974) became one of the largest overseas users of the F-51 Mustang in postwar years. Of ten Mustangs that made emergency landings in Sweden and were interned during the war, four aircraft (two P-51Bs and two P-51Ds) were pressed into Swedish service under the designation J26.

Even before V-E Day, Sweden ordered 50 P-51Ds from the United States, a figure that rose to 157, the first arriving in April 1945 and the last by March 1948. These, too, were designated J26. Thus, a total of 161

This J26 Mustang, *Flygvapen* serial 26020, alias F-51D 44-63992, of the Swedish Air Force appears to be a display aircraft (the twin booms of a Saab J21 pusher fighter are just barely visible in the background). The American Indian on horseback in the emblem on the fuselage, based on another version of the same picture by Knut Lindahl, signifies F16 wing (*Upplands Flygflottilj*), which Lindahl commanded, 1944-52. *Norman Taylor*

Uruguay operated a *grupo* of 25 F-51D Mustangs as fighter-bombers until 1960, when they were replaced by F-80C Shooting Stars. This F-51D, FAU 270 (44-63613), was acquired 4 December 1950 and is one of two survivors placed on display at Montevideo-Carrasco International Airport near Uruguay's capital following the type's withdrawal from service. This aircraft has since been returned to the United States. *Nery Mendiburu*

In war paint, NAA F-51D Mustang FAS 402 of the Salvadorian Air Force is seen at Illopango, ready to fight in El Salvador's war with Honduras. This aircraft, which once wore civil registry YS-210P, was one of at least fourteen Mustangs that fought in the war with Honduras and was the second ship (following the crash of the first) to wear the serial FAS 402. *Archie Baldocchi*

aircraft served in Sweden, assigned Flygvapen serial numbers 26001/26161. Twelve of these later became S26 photo-reconnaissance aircraft.

The Mustangs were purchased on three occasions, between April 1945 and the autumn of 1948, from surplus American stocks in England and Germany. The first planes were allocated to F16 wing in Uppsala and F4 wing in Froson. Later Mustangs were allocated to F21 wing in Lulea and finally to F8 wing in Barkarby, outside Stockholm.

Early in their service, Swedish Mustangs suffered a heavy toll in mishaps. In all, 60 of the 161 aircraft were lost due to crashes.

During 1952–54, equipping with Vampire jet fighters (Swedish designation J28) and with the Swedish-manufactured Saab J29 "Flying Barrel," Sweden disposed of most of its Mustangs. Sales abroad included 25 to Israel in 1952–53, 26 to Nicaragua in 1953, and 42 to the Dominican Republic in 1954.

Switzerland

Switzerland acquired 100 surplus F-51D Mustangs in 1948 while awaiting the delivery of De Havilland Vampire FB.Mk 6 jet fighters. Arrival of the Mustangs permitted retirement of the Flugwaffe's last surviving Messerschmitt Bf 109Es in 1949, and the Mustangs remained in service until 1956 when reequipment with the Vampire was completed.

Uruguay

Uruguay employed a squadron of F-51D Mustangs as fighter-bombers until 1960, when they were replaced by F-80C Shooting Stars. Fuerza Aerea Uruguay pilots underwent training in the United States and received the first of 25 aircraft (GAU 251/275) at Grupo No. 2's base at Durazno.

CHAPTER 5

P-51 Mustang at War (II)

When the Korean War began on 25 June 1950, most USAF fighters in the Far East were Lockheed F-80 Shooting Stars. Three squadrons of F-82 Twin Mustangs were also in the region.

To the astonishment of those who had already proclaimed the end of the Propeller Era, pilots began to complain that their jet-powered F-80s were wrong for the war now thrust upon them. The first phase of the war in that summer of 1950 required defending against an onslaught by North Korean forces supported by a second-rate air force equipped with prop-driven Yakovlev and Ilyushin warplanes. On one of the first missions to cover Americans withdrawing from Seoul, an F-80 pilot returned to his base in Japan and reported that he hadn't shot down a Yak-9 because it took his fast jet fighter a quarter of a mile to pull out of a high-speed turn and the Yak could turn on a dime.

When the first aerial victory was achieved—on 27 June 1950, as North Korean fighters swarmed over Seoul's Kimpo airfield—the victor was not one of the newfangled jets but, rather, a prop-driven F-82G Twin Mustang (46-383) of the 68th Fighter All-Weather

Punkin and *Oh-Kaye Baby* are RF-51D Mustang photo-reconnaissance ships belonging to the 45th TRS, the "Polka Dots," and are suitably dotted on propeller hub, wing tips, and elevator (but not rudder) tips. Though assigned to take pictures of the enemy, the RF-51Ds retained their standard armament of six .50cal machine guns and under-wing bomb pylons. *Larry Davis via JEM*

One of the first F-51D Mustangs to fight in the Korean War as part of the Dallas Provisional Squadron taxies on a rough strip at Taegu in the summer of 1950, with a little help from enlisted ground crew members who are assisting the pilot's forward vision. This provisional outfit was merged into the 51st Provisional Squadron and retained ten "Truman Gift" F-51s Mustangs that had been flown to Taegu by Col. Dean Hess and others. The Mustang quickly proved more suitable than jets for the demands of air-to-ground fighting in Korea. *Duane E. Biteman*

Squadron, piloted by Lt. William "Skeeter" Hudson with Lt. Carl Fraser as radar observer.

To be sure, the F-80 was a fine aircraft—in all, six North Korean planes were downed on 27 June and F-80s got three of them—but experts had concluded prematurely that the propeller era was over. Not only was the F-80 too fast for air-to-air maneuvering against North Korea's clunkers, it lacked the staying power of an F-82 or an F-51. F-80s had been assigned to the Far East as interceptors and, on the day the war began, lacked pylons to carry bombs or rockets in an air-to-ground role. Launching from the western Japanese island of Kyushu (or from Iwakuni, which was on the main island of Honshu), F-80s carried only .50cal (12.7mm) ammunition and could stay over a target for only 15min, while a Mustang could loiter for an hour and a Twin Mustang even longer.

To return to that first aerial victory of the war, a two-seat Yakovlev Yak-7U, radar observer Fraser remembers how his Twin Mustang got the kill:

"We were circling over Kimpo when two North Korean fighters came up out of some low clouds and started after Charlie Moran and Fred Larkins, who were flying in the number four [F-82G Twin Mus-

tang] in our flight. The North Korean's shooting was a little better than yesterday and they shot up Charlie's tail.

"My pilot, 'Skeeter' Hudson, slipped around and got on the tail of their flight leader. When the guy realized that we were there, he pulled up into some clouds and tried to shake us off. Fortunately, we were so close to him that we could see him even in the middle of the clouds. Our first burst hit the rear of the fuselage and knocked some pieces off. The Yak pilot racked it over in a steep turn to the right and we gave him another burst along the right wing. This set the gas tank on fire and took the right flap and aileron off. By this time we were so close we almost collided with him.

"I could clearly see the pilot turn around and say something to the observer. Then he pulled his canopy back and climbed out on the wing. Once again he leaned in and said something to the observer. But he was either scared or wounded as he never attempted to jump. The Yak pilot pulled the rip cord and the chute dragged him off the wing, just before the ship rolled over and went in.

"The whole action took place below 1,000ft [309m]. Later we found that Moran had evaded his Yak and stalled out. When he recovered he found himself dead astern of the other Yak and shot it down."

The 339th Fighter All-Weather Squadron, flying a racetrack pattern at higher altitude over Kimpo, saw the engagements below and heard Moran say that he was being shot at. Maj. James W. "Poke" Little quickly led a pair of F-82G Twin Mustangs down to the action and within minutes Little shot down one of the remaining North Korean fighters. Two other 339th pilots claimed victories but since no one could confirm them they were credited as probable kills. There is some evidence that the aerial victory by the 68th's 1st Lt. Charles B. Moran may, in fact, have occurred minutes—or at least seconds—ahead of Hudson's and that credit for being "first" should not have gone to Hudson.

Going to War

At the beginning of the Korean War, only a handful of Mustangs were in American units in the region and none belonged to "line" fighter squadrons. Steps were taken immediately to rush Mustangs to the Korean theater, but not every officer in the Far East approved. Some felt that the Mustang was not the best warplane in which to be fighting down near the deck. The Mustang was dangerously vulnerable to ground fire.

At Iwakuni on the main Japanese island of Honshu, the RAAF's No. 77 Squadron's F-51D Mustangs were ordered on 30 June 1950 to join the defense of South Korea. On 7 July, the Australians suffered their first combat loss when Squadron Leader G. Strout failed to return from an armed reconnaissance mis-

sion along the coast of North Korea. Strout's Mustang (A68-757) apparently was hit by ground fire while he was searching for targets of opportunity.

From the time the decision was made to go to war, American officers wanted more prop-driven fighters available to them. On 23 July 1950, the aircraft carrier USS *Boxer* (CV-21), serving as a cargo ship for the moment, arrived at Yokosuka, Japan, with 145 F-51D Mustang fighters for the USAF's command in the region, known as Far East Air Forces (FEAF) and pronounced to rhyme with "leaf." *Boxer* had made the Pacific crossing in a record 8 days, 16hr.

The Mustangs were a mixed blessing to the embattled Allies who were making a stand in a corner of Korea and facing the prospect of being pushed into the sea. True, the Mustang was more maneuverable and had greater endurance than the F-80 (at least until enlarged wing-tip tanks were developed for the F-80), but some airmen had doubts. Like their Navy counterparts, they viewed a liquid-cooled power-plant as vulnerable during low-level operations. For a time, serious consideration was given to fielding a squadron of Republic F-47N Thunderbolts (the former P-47), with air-cooled engines, in Korea. But the USAF did not have enough F-47s in inventory.

Although it took the Air Force a couple of weeks to get the first F-51 Mustang fighters into combat in Korea, the RF-51D photo-reconnaissance aircraft was in the conflict from the beginning. The 45th TRS, alias "Polka Dots," flew the RF-51D (originally desig-

nated F-6D) at Kimpo and other bases. Dale Frey's aircraft, here, is an RF-51D but wears the FF buzz number associated with fighters rather than the RF buzz number assigned to reconnaissance craft. *Dale Frey*

Jets to Props

Squadrons that converted from F-80C to F-51D included the 35th and 36th Fighter-Bomber Squadrons (FBS) of the 8th FBG; the 39th and 40th Fighter-Interceptor Squadrons (FIS) of the 35th Fighter-Interceptor Group (FIG), and the 12th and 67th FBS (of the 18th FBG).

The 40th FIS moved its Mustangs from Ashiya, Japan, to Pohang, on the east coast of Korea within the decreasing area of terrain still held by the UN allies. (Sixteen nations in the UN were to contribute troops to the defense of South Korea). Isolated from the UN Command by poor communications, the 40th found itself pitted against some 1,500 North Korean regulars and guerrillas. "Friendlies" nearby consisted of just a single South Korean regiment. The North Koreans were on the verge of capturing Pohang, and at the last minute, the 40th had to pack up and pull out.

In the months that followed, the UN allies were almost defeated by the North Koreans before the UN forces mounted an amphibious landing at Inchon and marched north. Ahead lay a new war with China.

Mustang Role

The F-51D Mustang was always at the forefront of the fighting. Mustangs were the first fighters to be engaged by the MiG-15—although neither ever shot the other down. Soon, the Mustang became part of the ROKAF, which had only been formed the previ-

On 5 August 1950, Maj. Louis J. Sebille, commander of the 67th FBS, led Mustangs against North Korean artillery and troops tucked into the bank of a river near Hamchang. Sebille was flying an F-51D Mustang (44-74394) when he sustained battle damage and sacrificed his life by diving into his target—his posthumous award becoming one of only four Medals of Honor received by US Air Force people in Korea. This rare portrait snapped over Northern Luzon, Philippines, in August 1948 shows Major Sebille flying another F-51D Mustang, *Nancy III* (44-74112), which belonged to another pilot, Ed Hodges. *Duane E. Biteman*

Loaded with 5in HVAR and wearing a diagonal stripe around the rear fuselage that usually identifies a squadron commander, a "Bout One" NAA F-51D Mustang (44-73592) heads off on a combat mission, passing tents like those occupied many who flew and worked on these fighters. *Duane E. Biteman*

An F-51D Mustang of the ROKAF taxies at Kimpo airfield in 1953. The Mustang was the first warplane operated by South Korea. At first, the only indigenous pilots available were Koreans who had flown with Japanese forces in World War II. Only after the war had been underway for more than a year did the first Korean pilots come to the United States for flight training. *Norman Green*

ous year (on 10 October 1949) with just 187 officers and 1,671 enlisted personnel, three T-6 trainers, and 13 liaison planes. This puny beginning of the ROKAF ignored a pre-war recommendation by Gen. Claire Chennault that the South Korean air arm be equipped with 100 planes, including 25 F-51 Mustangs. The Mustang came only after the onset of fighting. Lieutenant Colonel Duane E. (Bud) Biteman remembers early Mustang efforts with the ROKAF and with his own unit:

"As far as the South Korean air arm was concerned, President Truman specifically authorized the immediate transfer of ten F-51s to the totally underequipped ROKAF. Those ten Mustangs, gathered from wherever they could be found at US bases in Japan—remember, all of our fighter groups had converted to F-80s the year before, and [our] P-51s had been shipped out months before, so the only flyable '51s were those that had been retained by the fighter squadrons for towing targets for the jets' aerial gunnery practice. Their condition verified the rumor.

They were real dogs. Half of the instruments and navigation radios had been removed—after all, who needs those when the ships are used only in VFR [visual flight rules] and just going to and from a gunnery range. Unfortunately, those key pieces and parts were not replaced before sending the Mustangs to Korea. Major Dean Hess and his crew, code-named *Bout One Project*, flew those 51s to Taegu for delivery to the ROKAF, and one of their first steps was to paint the ROKAF markings to cover those of the USAF. Hess's people were supposed to train the ROKs, but since [the South Korean] pilots had never flown anything more sophisticated than a T-6, after a few frustrating attempts at leading inept pilots into combat, Hess and his people told the ROK pilots to stand aside, and the *Bout One* pilots flew all of their initial combat missions.

"At about the same time that *Bout One* was being formed in Japan, we at Clark Field in the Philippines were putting together a single volunteer squadron from amongst the most experienced '51 pilots of the three squadrons of the 18th Group; we were code-named *Dallas Provisional Squadron*. Because the 18th had long since become an operator of the F-80 rather than the '51, we had no airplanes; we were to collect those upon our arrival [around 10 July 1950]. But when we arrived at Taegu, there were no airplanes to be had, so it was decided that *Bout One* and the *Dallas*

Wing tanks everywhere. When loaded with fuel, the teardrop shape accommodated 62.5gal in its original version, or 108gal as shown here. It was also the container for napalm, the jellied gasoline employed during close-support strikes on ground troops. During the Korean War, with the comparatively small number of Mustangs committed to action, the USAF apparently never had difficulty with its supply line of wing tanks.

Provisional Squadron were to be merged under command of our Capt. Harry H. Moreland. Other pilots in our group included Capts. Howard C. (Scrappy) Johnson, Jerome R. (Jerry) Mau, and Clair W. Potter. We also had a dozen lieutenants. Lieutenants Daniel (Chappie) James and Don Bolt were to follow shortly.

"The *Bout One* pilots were given the choice of remaining with us in the new unit, or return[ing] with Dean Hess to Japan to scrounge additional pilots and equipment in order to establish his F-51 ROKAF training program that was based near Masan. Most of their pilots elected to remain with us and fight the war, rather than become involved in the training program with the ROKAF. When our two provisional units joined forces, we were renamed the 51st Provisional Squadron, and we retained the original ten 'Truman Gift' F-51s that had been flown to Taegu by Hess's people. We retained the 51st Provisional Squadron title until the 18th FBG and its 67th FBS moved north from Clark Field to rejoin the fray on

approximately 1 August 1950, when we were re-absorbed into the 18th and again renamed 12th FBS. We continued to fly the remainder of those ten original relics until the arrival of the *Boxer* with its load of wonderful, 'new,' completely equipped National Guard Mustangs."

Medal Mission

On 5 August 1950, Maj. Louis J. Sebille, commander of the newly-arrived 67th FBS/18th FBW, led a flight of Mustangs against North Korean artillery and troops tucked into the bank of a river near Hamchang. Sebille was flying an F-51D Mustang (44-74394).

Sebille's fighter-bomber pilots proceeded to help out friendly ground troops who faced overwhelming odds. Sebille made a bombing run and disgorged a pair of 500lb (227kg) bombs. Next, he banked sharply to circle the target and radioed his wingmen to make a strafing pass.

Now, furious ground fire sent shells careening around the Mustangs. Major Sebille's aircraft was hit. His wingman surveyed the damage, thought it serious, and advised him to return to safety at Taegu. Instead, Sebille again rolled in on the target and began strafing with his six .50cal (12.7mm) machine-guns. During this attack, Sebille apparently withstood additional damage, for he flew straight into the

The F-51D Mustang (left) was the combat aircraft flown by Australia's No. 77 Squadron during the occupation of Japan and the first months of the Korean War. As the war continued, the RAAF decided to replace the P-51 with the British-made Gloster Meteor F.Mk VIII (right). Both were effective in the air-to-ground mission but neither was able to do battle in the air with the MiG-15. *Michael P. Curphey*

A typical view of conditions at K-46 airfield near Wonju, Korea, where the 18th FBW battled frigid, near-Arctic conditions in winter and sloshed through the mud in summer. Pilots lived in tents and made furnishings from the boxes used as containers for 5in rockets. Mechanics worked on the F-51D Mustangs out of doors, under the most primitive conditions. *Devol Brett*

Captain De Bruler of the 12th FBS/18th FBG, strikes up a pose in front of F-51D Mustang 44-74846 at K-10 Chinhae air base in South Korea. Members of the 18th FBW fought their war in Korea at low altitude and often lived at crude airfields that were muddy in the spring and frozen solid in the winter. The 18th FBW operated Mustangs in Korea from an early juncture in the war in 1950 until early 1953 when the wing belatedly converted to another fighter from the same manufacturer, the F-86F Sabre. *Ralph H. Saltsman, Jr.*

concentration of enemy troops where his Mustang exploded in their midst. For sacrificing his life to help friendly ground troops, Maj. Louis J. Sebille posthumously became the first USAF member and the first flier in Korea to be awarded the Medal of Honor.

September 1950 began sadly for the Australians when No. 77 Squadron's Pilot Officer W. P. Harrop, coming home from escorting B-29s to Pyongyang, crashed his F-51D Mustang (A68-753) 5mi from Taegu, a "divert" airfield on this day but one to which the RAAF was to transfer from Iwakuni within the month. On 3 September 1950, No. 77's skipper, Wing Commander Lou Spence, was lost in his F-51D Mustang (A68-809) while attacking the town of Angangni with rockets and machine gun fire. Spence's slot was filled by Squadron Leader R. G. Creswell. Like

many of the hard-fighting Australians, including some who were sergeant-pilots, Creswell had seen heavy action in the Second World War.

In November 1950, Chinese troops entered the conflict. So, too, did swept-wing MiG-15 jet fighters stationed in Manchuria but flown, at first, largely by Soviet pilots. On 1 November 1950, F-51 Mustangs were engaged by six swept-wing jet fighters that lashed out at them from across the Yalu River, the border between North Korea and China, which Allied pilots were forbidden to cross.

At FEAF's hard-working intelligence shop, experts knew of huge, modern airfields on the Chinese side of the Yalu at Antung, Tatangkou, and Fen Cheng. But intelligence analysts, and indeed Gen. Douglas MacArthur, knew little of what was happening in China and even less about the swept-wing jet fighters reported by the Mustang pilots. The MiG-15 had arrived.

On 16 November 1950, Australia's No. 77 Squadron moved its F-51D Mustangs from Pohang north to the airfield at Yonpo, known as Konan North. It was becoming clear that an apparent UN victory in Korea was, in fact, going to be nothing of the sort, and the intrepid Australians found themselves flying repeated sorties against swarms of enemy tanks and vehicles moving not north, but *south*, along the highways coming down from Manchuria. It was dirty fighting, and the Mustangs, tarrying over the enemy at low altitude with full ordnance, often took hits. In weeks ahead, the Chinese were to virtually overrun the airfield, forcing No. 77 to withdraw under fire and re-locate, once more, at Pusan. Throughout the war, the squadron continued to have back-up and maintenance facilities at Iwakuni.

South Africans

The Union of South Africa, in those days a member of the UN and of the British Commonwealth, supported UN action in Korea with one squadron, No. 2 "Flying Cheetahs." The first operation carried out by the SAAF in Korea occurred on 19 November 1950 when Commandant Theron and Captain Lipawsky took off from K-9 airfield to bomb and strafe communist supply lines. The aircraft recovered at K-24, the name assigned to an airstrip at Pyongyang in North

Korea, to be followed later in the day by Capt. J. F. O. Davis and Capt. W. J. J. Badenhorst. The remaining Mustangs of No. 2 Cheetah Squadron moved up to occupied Pyongyang and the South Korean squadron commenced to operate from North Korean soil.

Conditions at K-24 were primitive with the advance party living in tents in bitter winter conditions. No transport was available and all equipment had to be manhandled. The mess hall consisted of an old former North Korean Air Force hangar built of wood with gaping holes through which the freezing wind whistled fiercely, while the dirt floor was damp and cold. The one short runway was soft and rough, which made operating from it very difficult. Not surprisingly, the South Africans, like American pilots who flew the Mustang, watched the contrails of jet jocks high up in the stratosphere, thought of the hot meals and clean beds available to them, and viewed the jet pilots with some disdain.

The F-51D Mustangs of South Africa's No. 2 Cheetah Squadron lost their first aircraft on 5 Decem-

At frigid, mucky K-46 airfield near Wonju in South Korea in the late fall of 1951, Mustang pilots loiter around Capt. Devol (Rock) Brett's F-51D Mustang (44-14268), alias *Noherohere*, of the 39th FIS/18th FBW. Brett's wife Mamie had urged him to go off to the war and do his job but not to be a hero, hence the airplane nickname, perhaps the only time he didn't listen to her. Left to right: an unidentified crew chief; Lieutenant Davis (first name unknown); Maj. Jack Davis (no relation), 39th FIS commander; and Captain Brett. *Devol Brett*

Captain Devol Brett (right) of the 18th FBW stands with a crew chief in front of his F-51D Mustang in Korea. *Devol Brett*

ber 1950 when rockets fired by Captain Davis struck a railway truck loaded with explosives, which blew up with a terrific explosion, and Davis was temporarily knocked unconscious. His No. 2, Captain Lipawsky, covered him and called for help. An American L-5 Sentinel liaison craft arrived at the scene and the pilot made a skillful landing on a narrow road adjacent to the downed Mustang. The observer, a Captain Millet, gave up his seat to Davis. This was an outstanding act of bravery as the area was surrounded by enemy troops, and when the L-5 later returned to the scene, Millet had disappeared and no trace of him could be found. Only much later, on a separate sortie, Millet was found and picked up.

The fashionably attired Mustang jock of the Korean conflict. Major Duane E. (Bud) Biteman of the 18th FBW wears a web belt with sidearm, slick pilot's wings indicating that he has not yet attained command-pilot status, and the wheel hat introduced in 1949. The new, blue hat puzzled USAF fliers because, while the equivalent Army hat was designed to have its brim spit-shined, the USAF model was not. In the background is an F-51D Mustang of the 12th FBS/18th FBW. *Duane E. Biteman*

Later in the month, the South Africans were notified that they would move from Pyongyang back to K-10 airfield at Chinhae, in the southernmost part of South Korea. In due course, other 18th FBW Mustangs operating from K-46, near Wonju, also redeployed to K-10. Chinhae was the field they would occupy for the next two years.

By 1951, the Chinese were fully in the war and were unleashing a nine-division main thrust southward driving toward Seoul and beyond. Once they'd seized the capital, they pressed south. Much farther south at Chinhae, where F-51D Mustangs of the 18th FBW labored around the clock, Col. P. M. J. McGregor of the South African contingent wrote, "It was not an uncommon sight to see torch lights around aircraft parked on the flight line at night as fitters, riggers, and electricians were feverishly engaged in checking each aircraft for the next day's operations, while the armorers loaded the machine-guns and bombed up and fitted rockets to the aircraft scheduled for the first mission next morning."

The Mustang pilots paid a heavy price. Among the South Africans, Lt. W. E. Wilson was hit by small-arms fire on 2 February 1950 and bailed out over the sea only to disappear. Second Lieutenant D. R. Leah was killed on 7 February when his aircraft was seen to strike the ground while strafing enemy vehicles on the road south of Yonhung. On 15 February Lieu-

F-51D Mustangs of the 18th FBW on the line in Korea in 1952. *Devol Brett*

"Cobra in the Sky," it was called by some. The 39th FBS was one of four flying units in the 18th FBW and was a user of the F-51D Mustang from early in the Korean War until early 1953. This sign and these buildings reflect conditions at K-46 airfield near Wonju, which one pilot called "a real sporting place to fly." There were no hangars, no barracks buildings, and few amenities. *Devol Brett*

tenant Doveton's aircraft was shot down by ground fire while he was strafing enemy positions in the Kaesong area and he was killed. On 1 March, the Cheetahs flew 32 sorties and established a new 18th FBW record, destroying seven vehicles, two tanks, and an unknown number of troops, but the F-51D Mustang flown by Captain Bandenhorst was shot down and he was killed while Lieutenant Ruiter was also hit by enemy fire and disappeared into the sea.

Recce Mustangs

One final American outfit in Korea flying the Mustang was the 45th TRS "Polka Dots," activated in 1951 as part of the 67th TRG. The RF-51D reconnaissance aircraft flown by the Polka Dots carried out some of the most dangerous missions of the war. Casualties were high.

In May 1951, Australia's No. 77 Squadron withdrew from Pusan to Iwakuni to complete its transition to Gloster Meteor F.Mk VIII twin-engine jet fighters (plus a pair of two-seat Meteor F.Mk VII trainers) as replacements for its battle-weary F-51D Mustangs.

On 20 June 1951, the Mustang came up against communist warplanes for a rare, air-to-air fracas. Documents from the period gave credit to Mustang pilots for four aerial victories, although none of the four, apparently, was made official. Lieutenant Colonel Ralph D. Saltsman of the 18th FBW found himself shooting at a rare Ilyushin Il-10 prop-driven fighter-bomber when he couldn't even see it. The USAF's highly classified *Air Intelligence Digest* identified Saltsman's adversary as an Ilyushin Il-2 Shturmovik and listed it as a confirmed kill, although both Saltsman and the official record make it a "probable."

Devoid of squadron markings, freshly painted, fully "hung" with wing tanks and bomb pylons, these F-51D Mustangs look as if they've just rolled out of the factory. In truth, these Mustangs have just received rear-echelon refurbishing in Japan and are now ready to be returned to fighting squadrons in Korea. By the time of the Korean War, the Mustang had been out of production for nearly five years.

An F-51D Mustang of the RAAF's No. 77 Squadron taxiing at Kimpo air base near Seoul.

F-51D Mustang 44-63674 flies over Mount Fuji near Tokyo during the Korean era. *via Robert Esposito*

Saltsman remembers, "I heard that a classified mission was planned for early morning takeoff from K-16 [Seoul airport], so I flew up to that base from K-10 [Chinhae] at about 5:00 A.M. to participate. Apparently, our intelligence agencies had learned that the North Koreans planned to invade the island of Senmido, which was about 3mi [5km] off the western coast of Korea and 75mi [120km] south of the Yalu River. Allied forces apparently had a radar installation on the island.

"I was leading BAKER Flight in the squadron led by Capt. Ed Rackham. As we arrived over the area at about 7:00 A.M. at 12,000ft [3,715m], we spotted six enemy aircraft of the Shturmovik type, circling below us.

"Rackham told me to attack them. When we reached the trailing aircraft at about 6,000ft [1,858m], the rear gunner opened fire on me. I took a position astern and below the aircraft, which appeared to be an Il-2, thus positioning my aircraft out of the gunner's view. Raising my nose I fired about 800 rounds of .50cal [12.7mm] into the bottom of the enemy aircraft.

"It started to smoke. But as I repeated the attack, my windscreen became covered with oil, which limited my visibility to a small part of the left side.

"Unable to maintain visual contact with the enemy aircraft, I broke off the attack. Meanwhile my wingman had left his position at the initial attack and could not be located. I joined-up with the returning aircraft, finding that I could see better with my canopy open. We landed back at K-16 at about 7:45 A.M., this concluding a very successful Mission No. 1801."

98

RF-51D Mustang 44-84852 of the 45th TRS "Polka Dots" nick-named *My Arline* at Kimpo air base in 1952. *Robert Esposito*

General Hoyt S. Vandenberg, chief of staff of the USAF, visits the P-51 Mustang-equipped 35th FG during the Korean War era. *via Robert Esposito*

That same day. First Lieutenant J. B. Harrison was credited with an Ilyushin kill according to the 18th FBW's newspaper, *The Truckbuster*. "After 15 minutes over the target," Harrison was quoted, "the flight covering the bottom called in and reported that there was [*sic*] six bogies below. The squadron commander told the flight to go down and identify the aircraft and the battle was on.

"As I started to take my element down, the enemy saw us coming and turned into us. By that time my flight leader, Maj. W. F. MacGregor, was making his pass on the enemy aircraft.

"One enemy aircraft turned right into me and I was able to get on his tail and stayed there until his engine caught on fire. Then he rolled over and bailed out.

"The enemy pilot must have just completed training for he sure was 'green,'" concluded Harrison. In addition to Saltsman and Harrison, Capts. Bruce R. Clark and Landell Hames were also credited at the time with shooting down aircraft identified at the time as Il-2s.

Continuing Conflict

The NAA F-51D Mustang continued to be the premier fighter of the war in the prop-driven category, at least in the eyes of the many who flew it. Operating out of K-16 air base on an island in the Han River at Seoul, 1st Lt. James F. Byers of the 12th FBS/18th FBW flew a difficult Mustang sortie in September 1951. Byers remembers the hectic pace of the war at that time:

"It had been a busy day with plenty of targets. Just before dark, we were again scrambled to a target near a small village called Naesokyo, north of Chorwon and east of the Imjin River. Lieutenant Wyatt was the flight leader. Lieutenant Shoemaker was on his first mission was in the number two slot, I was number three, and Lieutenant Morrison was number four.

"A tac-recce aircraft had spotted a large amount of equipment dug in along a hillside, in revetments. Our job was to shoot 'em up. All we had were rockets and .50cals [12.7mm]. We had no bombs and no napalm.

"We dived in on the target and were met by a heavy barrage of small arms and automatic weapons fire. We made several passes trying to get something to burn. Nothing! It was just about dark and without proper ordnance, we decided to head for home. On the way back to base, we figured that the way the area had been defended, that it must be very important to the enemy.

"Upon landing, we immediately went to our intelligence officer, Captain Macgloughlin, with the suggestion that we should go back at first light with two flights carrying air bursting VT bombs [i.e., bombs with 'variable time' fuzes, a type of proximity fuse that detonates at varying distances from the target, usually producing an airburst that takes out enemy personnel within a wide radius] and two flights with napalm. The VT bombs would knock

F-51 Mustangs of the 39th FS during the Korean conflict. *via Robert Esposito*

An F-51D Mustang of the 40th FBS in Korea. *via Robert Esposito*

down the flak and then the Mustangs with the napalm could get in for a good job with a minimum of enemy counter-action.

"Approval was quickly given. We took off in the early A.M. with me leading the 12th [squadron's] flight. Right behind us was the 67th [squadron's] flight, which carried the VT's. The final two flights were from the 39th Squadron and they had napalm.

"We took our dives from 7,500ft [2,322m] and dropped the VTs. Just as we started, I gave the word for the 39th guys to start in from the west, on the deck, and spread the napalm. They did the finest job of burning up equipment I have ever seen. They never received any enemy fire as the VT's had done the job. The mission went so smooth and was such a success, that it brought back memories of [my World War II squadron] in Europe."

Well, *most* of the time things went smoothly, but F-51D Mustang pilot Byers got into his share of scrapes, too.

"I always felt that the Mustang could hold its own in a scrape with the MiG. If you could keep the fight down low, you could turn inside of him and the '51 had more firepower.

"We'd just finished attacking some small bridges around Sinanju. The objectives were taken out with a minimum of ordnance, so we started to recce the roads in hopes of finding some targets. We heard the 12th [squadron] finish up and start their recce, and moments later we heard the 39th [squadron] Mustangs do the same. Wally Parks had the final flight of

39th aircraft, and as he pulled up off the target, he was bounced by MiG-15s. Four of them!

"Parks was a scrapper. So he took them on and called for help. We headed back to the target area as quickly as we could, to find the MiGs gone and Parks heading home with three aircraft in his flight. It seems that Parks and two of his pilots had stayed down low and turned inside the MiG's getting in some good shots while the fourth pilot had tried to run for it—with the MiG flying right up his tail. The MiG-15 opened fire and disintegrated the Mustang with one burst. The entire fight was over in a flash as the MiGs were burning up precious fuel at that low altitude."

K-46 Airfield

"A very sporty place to fly out of," remembered Maj. Devol "Rock" Brett, speaking of K-46 airfield near Wonju, sometimes known as Hoengsong. Brett's was the West Point class of 1945, which had missed the big war and was to give up many of its sons in this smaller one. He had 1,500hr in Thunderbolts, 600hr in Mustangs, and was the only regular officer in his wing. Most of the men were citizens, not professional soldiers: voluntary and involuntary call-ups, no longer all that young, the average in their mid-twenties, most with families back home. At K-46, they slogged in the mud, froze in the fierce wind howling down through the mountains, and lived in tents that had no floors or walls until the men constructed them from rocket boxes.

Using the call sign MONGOOSE, F-51D Mustangs of the 18th wing pressed the attack on North Korea's rail system and flew armed reconnaissance, which meant a search for any target that popped up, often a convoy of oxcarts carrying ammunition. Brett's plane (44-14268) wore the nickname *Noherohere* in cartoon-style red letters: his wife had asked him to "be good, but don't be a hero," and his three-year old had repeated the behest.

The toughest missions were near the enemy capital: "The flak around Pyongyang East was thick enough to walk on." The targets of opportunity were often spotted north of the bomb line by RF-51D Mustangs, call sign HAMMER, and closer to the front lines by LT-6G Texans, call sign MOSQUITO. Brett sometimes led as many as 36 Mustangs on one mission, typically carrying two 500lb (227kg) bombs with delayed nose fuses, six high-velocity aircraft rockets (HVAR) with three on each wing, and a full load of .50cal (12.7mm) ammunition. Brett never ceased to marvel at the citizen soldiers who flew and fought with him, including one who seemed destined to be cut to shreds by a Mustang propeller.

Lieutenant Frederick Rockmacher, like Brett, a member of the wing's 39th squadron, was Brett's archetype for the ordinary man who rose to the occasion: "He had the name Rocky painted on his helmet but he was easygoing and nervous, nothing macho about him. He came from New York. His mom and dad owned a stationery store. He hated combat, was scared to death, but he always went. He never aborted. He never complained."

Coming back from a mission with night closing in, Rockmacher's F-51D flight experienced a "radio out" situation in which communications were glitched, pilots couldn't talk to each other, and there were problems igniting the flame pots along the primitive runway. "He'd known he was coming back with darkness a bigger threat than the North Koreans," remembered Brett. "There was confusion in the landing pattern. They'd swapped the flight lead because of the `radio out` situation." Rockmacher lowered his gear, dodged the peaks around K-46, and settled into his approach.

Because of the communications glitch, and it was no one's fault, really, another pilot, Eugene Z. Mazurak was supposed to be landing behind Rockmacher to his left but, instead, was touching down directly *behind* Rockmacher. When the first Mustang slowed, Gene Mazurak slammed on his brakes in the second, but it was too late. Mazurak's faster-moving aircraft caught up with Rockmacher's and climbed on top of it—as Brett recalls, "like two dogs copulating." Mazurak's propeller chewed pieces of Rockmacher's airplane up and sent shards of aluminum flying everywhere.

The second Mustang, propeller still turning, still cutting up metal amid an ear-shattering din, with the spinning prop blade just 6in behind Rockmacher's head. The noise was deafening. The spinner was actually *above* Rockmacher's head, pinning him in his seat. Other pilots reached the scene and tried to help. Brett saw gasoline spilling everywhere around the two Mustangs, which now looked more like one and a half Mustangs, and was certain some damn fool was going to light up.

"Don't light a cigarette!" Brett ordered. He clambered up on the wing saw Rockmacher looking up, in

F-51D Mustang flight line. *via Robert Esposito*

When things go wrong, they really go wrong. A South African F-51D Mustang pilot of No. 2 Cheetah Squadron lost control of his aircraft on takeoff at Chinhae, Korea, in the spring of 1951, apparently because he was inexperienced in the Mustang and did not understand how torque pulled on the airplane. Fully loaded with bombs and rockets, the pilot veered into 25 parked aircraft of the 18th FBW. The resulting impact and fire destroyed several aircraft and killed the pilot. *Pancho Pasqualicchio*

the darkness and confusion, at the now-halted propeller and the spinner above his head. "It's me," Rockmacher said, as if there could be a possible way for it to be someone else. "Get me out of here. I'm scared of a fire."

It was Rocky's lucky day—or night. Not long afterward, Brett accompanied Rockmacher on his 100th mission and watched this citizen-soldier end his tour and go home. Mazurak deserves a lot of credit for pulling back the prop early.

Cheetahs

In December 1952, the SAAF's No. 2 Squadron, the Flying Cheetahs, turned in their F-51D Mustangs. The Cheetahs could look back at sacrifice and achievement while flying the propeller-driven fighters as part of the 18th FBW (since November 1950).

The Cheetahs flew 95 F-51Ds, purchased from USAF stocks and wearing SAAF numbers 301 through 396. No. 325 was lost on a delivery flight from Japan, and was not placed on SAAF strength. When innovative ground crews put together a complete airframe from three partial wrecks, the serial number 325 was finally used. Not many of the Mustangs carried names on the nose; recorded names include 318 *Shy Talk*, 326 *Papasan*, 369 *My Boy Alan Cuckoo Ii*, 377 *Maureens Joy*, 385 *Bonnie Pam*, 388 *Amandie*, and 395 *Sherdana*. Two others, numbers unknown, were named *Rosalie* and *Bugs*.

Seventy-four SAAF Mustangs were written off or lost in Korea. Thirty-four pilots were missing or killed in action. The Cheetahs flew 2,890 missions and 10,597 sorties. Now, the South Africans prepared to go into action with F-86F Sabre fighter-bombers.

Scarcely noticed amid all this, the last combat mission by a Mustang was flown on 23 January 1953. Plans were already under way for the 18th FBW to convert to Sabres.

CHAPTER 6

Pilot Talk (II)

Looking back on our air-to-ground bombing, strafing, napalming, and rocket fire in Italy, France, Germany, and Korea, I sometimes think of the Book of Common Prayer version of the Sixth Commandment, which goes, Thou Shalt Do No Murder.

I remember a spring day in 1951 when I had to decide whether to execute three strangers to prevent the possible killing of a junior officer for whose safety I had become responsible. If they killed Pancho [Capt. Robert B. "Pancho" Pasqualicchio, pilot of an F-51D Mustang nicknamed *Ol' Nadsob* (45-11742) with the 67th FBS/18th FBW], there was no place they would be safe from our retaliatory machine-gun fire. But that was no help in reaching a decision.

At that time the Han River was the front line west of Seoul. We had complete control of the sky over the parts of South Korea still occupied by the North Korean invaders. Our usual flight missions were to disrupt enemy transportation and to destroy supplies.

We flew low-level fighter-bomber sorties using F-51D liquid-cooled Mustang airplanes built during World War II for high-altitude aerial combat. Our gravest danger was from rifle fire or shrapnel puncturing the cooling system. Coolant would leak through any small hole, causing the engine to overheat. A pilot who radioed that his engine gauge was reading too high usually had to parachute or crash-land.

Since there were no enemy planes within a hundred miles of us, we didn't need the mutual protection provided by the eight-, twelve-, and sixteen-ship formations designed for aerial combat. Using flights of only two airplanes we covered more territory with fewer pilots. But if anything happened to the leader of a two-plane flight, his wingman in the second plane often was a new pilot without enough experience to handle the emergency.

Low-level Sortie

On one such two-ship mission a few miles north of the Han River, my wingman and I were looking for suitable targets when there was a call on the unit's VHF radio frequency:

"GEMSTONE YELLOW One. Coolant trouble. I'll try to make it to the rice paddies near the river. Out."

I recognized the voice of a young captain named Pancho, a nickname given by other pilots of his home state ANG squadron. We had never flown together. Because of some ten years difference in our ages and considerable difference in military rank we had never socialized at the club. But I had noticed his bouncy enthusiasm and knew he was respected as a competent pilot by his peers.

GEMSTONE was the squadron call sign that week. As the leader of Green Flight my call sign was GEMSTONE GREEN ONE. My wingman was GEMSTONE GREEN TWO. Pancho, GEMSTONE YELLOW ONE, was leading one of the other flights patrolling the area west of Seopul. Knowing that GEMSTONE YELLOW must be near us, I radioed to get their location:

"Roger, GEMSTONE YELLOW ONE. Tell us where you are and GEMSTONE GREEN will cover you. Out."

Pancho's wingman was glad to turn the responsibility over when we reached where he was circling. The silver aluminum aircraft had skidded to a stop after smearing a muddy streak through three hundred yards of rice plants. Mud walls dividing the rice fields into shallow ponds had been flattened by the crash landing.

The forced landing had been successful. The fact the plane had not caught fire showed that Pancho had

This portrait may make the F-51D appear to be somewhat more crowded than it really is. Note sliding canopy, rudder, and elevator details in this close-up. Those who like to compare wartime fighters have said that the P-47 Thunderbolt looked like it came from an iron works, while the P-51 appeared as if it had been crafted by artisans. A touch of grace is evident in virtually every detail.

An F-51D Mustang fighter pilot of the 18th FBW poses in front of his aircraft at Chinhae airfield, South Korea, in 1951. Robert C. Brown of the wing's 67th FBS found himself confronting a dilemma: what to do about unknown individuals approaching a downed Mustang pilot on the ground? Even at low level where the 18th operated during the Korean War, it was not always possible to distinguish friend from foe. *Pancho Pasqualicchio*

NAA F-51D Mustangs of the 12th FBS/18th FBW, on the dirt-covered parking ramp at Chinhae, South Korea, in late 1951. The shark teeth are unique to this squadron. The tail number of the aircraft at left front (44-74392) is a non-standard presentation. Had the number been painted on the Mustang according to the standard format, it would appear here as 474392. *Pancho Pasqualicchio*

F-51D Mustang fighter-bombers at Chinhae, South Korea. These Mustangs are loaded with yellow, 108gal napalm containers for air-to-ground action against enemy troops. On just such a mission, the pilot of Robert C. Brown's narrative was shot down and threatened by people on the ground. Air Force officers wanted to use the F-47D Thunderbolt in Korea instead of the P-51, feeling the former aircraft would be better in air-to-ground fighting, but not enough Thunderbolts were available. *Pancho Pasqualicchio*

shut down the electrical system and closed the fuel line leading to the engine before crashing. Except for a couple of bent propeller blades, the Mustang looked intact.

After radioing for a search and rescue helicopter, I joined the other two pilots to give Pancho the protection of three planes spaced 120deg apart in a wide overhead circle. We flew above him at 1,000ft, low enough for observation but high enough for reasonable protection from enemy fire. We could use our machine guns against anyone on the ground who seemed to threaten the damaged airplane.

Circling to the left, we followed each other in a deadly serious game of Follow the Leader. Throttling back to fly slowly made it easy to see details of the area around Pancho and stretched out the time before we would have to return to our base for refueling.

We had a clear view across miles of bright green plants and muddy water. Nobody was working in the rice paddies. A village half a mile away seemed deserted until ten or twelve men started across the fields toward the plane. We couldn't tell whether the men were peasants or whether—as had happened before in that war—they were enemy soldiers disguised as peasants.

Pilot's Dilemma

Our problem was to keep the men from getting too close to GEMSTONE YELLOW ONE. If they were friendly South Korean peasants overrun by the North Koreans, the helicopter rescue under way made their help unnecessary. If they were North Korean soldiers trying to capture or kill him, we had to keep them from getting within shooting distance.

Cautioning the other pilots to fire well in front of the men, I called for warning bursts across their line of advance as each of us in turn came into firing position.

With each burst the Koreans stopped for a few moments, but then continued toward the plane during the seconds none of us were in position to shoot. Our shooting slowed their progress, but it would not be enough to keep the men from reaching Pancho before the rescue helicopter arrived.

Several times the pattern repeated itself. One of us in position of fire would bring them to a stop, which lasted only while the shooting continued. The men then walked forward until the next airplane was in position to shoot. When that airplane put a burst of machine gun fire across their path, they stopped—but only while it was in firing position.

Our shooting did discourage some of them. By the two-thirds mark only three men continued to press forward.

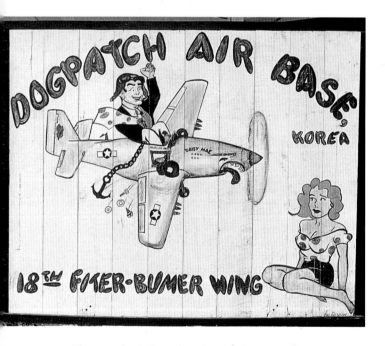

The accommodations where the 18th FBW lived were anything but the Ritz. The sign at Chinhae, South Korea, is lifted from Al Capp's famous L'il Abner comic strip, as is the name of the strip's heroine, Daisy Mae. Americans liked the comic strip but hated the place. A favorite expression written on latrine walls at Chinhae was usually reduced to the abbreviation IHTFP, which means (approximately), "I hate this place." *Pancho Pasqualicchio*

If the three men intended to harm Pancho, the surest way to protect him was to shoot to kill before they reached him. I couldn't act on the fact they weren't brandishing weapons. They could easily have guns concealed in their clothing.

If they were friendly South Korean farmers wanting to help, it would be a terrible thing to wound or kill them.

I discussed the problem with the two younger pilots. The decision was mine to make, so I wasn't asking for their approval. It wasn't that I wanted their advice. Partly I was thinking out loud, partly I wanted to get any evidence they had about whether the three men were hostile soldiers or good Samaritans who didn't realize we couldn't tell the difference from the air.

Should I kill three Koreans who might be trying to help?

Or should I risk the life of our of our pilots?

I knew what I would want done if I were the pilot on the ground. But my wife and I had no children at that time. What was right for me was not necessarily right for Pancho.

Fortunately for the Koreans and for me, Pancho was able to make the decision.

In addition to the possibility of flying into a mountain, smashing into a large tree, or cartwheeling through ditches, the dangers of a crash landing include fire. Because an electrical spark can ignite gasoline fumes, key steps in preparing for a crash are disconnecting the battery and turning off such electrical equipment as lights and radios.

When Pancho's F-51D Mustang first came to rest after skidding through the mud and shallow water, one of his first moves was to check for evidence of leaking fuel. Even a smoothly-executed wheels-up landing can result in ruptured tanks. As the minutes went by without any smell of gasoline he decided to risk the danger of fire. Putting the battery switch into the On position he was pleased to find that his radio and its antenna had survived the accident.

Lucky call

As a result of his successful gamble with fire, Pancho interrupted our discussion about the intentions of the approaching Koreans.

"GEMSTONE GREEN ONE, this is Pancho. I think you're right. They're probably friendly. I've got my .45. Let them keep coming. I'll get out on the wing. With the fuselage between us. I can keep them covered."

While we continued to circle, the Koreans reached the plane. It took a lot of shouting and gestures from Pancho before the men gave up trying to get him to accept their help and returned to their village.

A rescue helicopter arrived 15min later. I've always been thankful that Pancho was able to make his own decision. He may have saved me from 40

Captain Robert B. "Pancho" Pasqualicchio, whose last name was deemed too long to be painted on the red canopy rails, prepares to taxi out at Chinhae in his F-51D Mustang nicknamed *Ol' Nadsob* (45-11742) with the 67th FBS/18th FBW. Several people have asked Captain Pasqualicchio the significance of the nickname on his aircraft, but his lips are sealed. *Pancho Pasqualicchio*

years of fearing that I had committed murder.

Underlining how much I consider Pancho to have been the primary actor in the drama, I wrote him my heartfelt regret that our military policy doesn't provide for awarding him the Medal of Honor for having let us put him in mortal danger.

Ed Hodges, 67th FBS/18th FBW

My outfit was one of the first to operate the Mustang in Korea. The 67th, along with the 12th FBS, was withdrawn from Clark Field, the Philippines, when the Korean War started. In July and August 1950, we converted from F-80Cs to F-51s to join the conflict.

We picked our aircraft up at Johnson AB near Tokyo where they had been offloaded from the aircraft carrier USS *Boxer* (CV-21). I understand they were withdrawn by twos and threes from Reserve and National Guard units in the states. We flew them down to Ashiya AB, Japan, firing the guns in the water near Shimonoseki Strait to see if they were any-

where near bore-sighted. They weren't. Even worse, most of the barrels were burned out and tracers came out in a corkscrew trajectory.

The next day, while our ground troops were working on the aircraft and loading ammo, our squadron CO [commanding officer] Louis J. Sebille, ops officer Maj. Arnold "Moon" Mullins, and I flew F-80Cs on an armed recce mission in the Masan area of the Naktong perimeter.

When we got back to Ashiya, Lou, Moon, and I led the first F-51 flights back over the fray. Lou Sebille was killed on August 6.

He was not only my squadron commander, he was my mentor and the closest friend I ever had in my 28-plus years of service. I was never able to allow myself to be that intimately associated with a fellow pilot after his death. I had flown the previous day (early morning) on his wing, and we had spent the entire day before on a Jeep trip from Ashiya to Itazuke and return arranging shipment of some F-51 spares we'd located there. I was napping under the parachute rack when Lou left on his final mission. I awoke as he stepped over me and started to get up when I saw it was the CO, but he shook his head and said, "Don't get up, Ed. I'll see you later." When I returned from my second mission that day, I learned that not only Lou but our senior flight commander, Capt. Bob Howell, had been lost.

In Korea in September 1950 are (left to right) an Army liaison officer and F-51D Mustang pilots Ross Cree and Ed Hodges. Both pilots belong to the 67th FBS whose commander, Maj. Louis Sebille, was posthumously awarded the Medal of Honor after losing his life on an early Korean War combat mission. Cree probably saved Hodges' life, unintentionally, by lending him an ill-fitting back-pack parachute that opened faster than Hodges' own parachute would have done—a critical factor in a bailout from 700ft. *Edward Hodges*

I flew more missions, and saw others lost. A pilot named Don Bolt whom we all liked and admired—though we knew he had weaknesses in flying—was shot down, got out of his aircraft safely, but was killed before we could get help to him. In many ways, this low-level, air-to-ground fighting was rougher than my World War II experience as a pilot of the P-47 Thunderbolt.

The second of October 1950 proved to be the final day of mortal life for an able F-51D Mustang pilot of our 67th FBS, 1st Lt. Donald D. Bolt. The year before the war, Bolt had been grounded in an Air Force economy move. Given a chance to be put on inactive duty, he'd soldiered on, instead, giving excellent performance in a ground job. He returned to flying during the conflict, but one of his most important jobs was on the ground—ramrodding the paperwork for the Medal of Honor citation for

Sebille. Bolt almost single-handedly overcame resistance in Fifth Air Force and FEAF headquarters to get the recommendation for the medal passed on to Washington. Don Bolt's last day, as described by our fellow 67th FBW pilot Lt. Col. Duane E. Biteman, is typical of the grit and frustration of this dirty little war we were fighting:

"Don flew a pre-dawn mission to Pyongyang, North Korea's capital. His flight was almost to the target when the sun crept up. His airplane was hit in the engine by ground fire and he was able to glide just clear of a low ridge of hills east of the city before having to belly-in on a small, open rice field that was surrounded by a mile-wide ring of trees. After the Mustang came to a stop, Bolt jumped quickly out of the cockpit, onto the wing, then started running across the dry rice paddies toward the nearest trees. He stopped abruptly, after covering about a hundred feet, and ran quickly back to the far side of his crippled airplane, ducking low as he ran.

"He pointed his arm toward the trees, and [his] flight leader could see enemy troops jumping out of a truck alongside the trees. The leader made a strafing pass, firing his machine guns between Don's aircraft and the North Korean truck, making sure *not to hit the troops* [Biteman's emphasis] but, at the same time, giving them notice to stay back and leave Bolt's airplane alone.

"[The flight leader] called MELLOW Control [Fifth Air Force operations control, located at Taegu] for help, giving Don's position and the fact that he appeared to be uninjured. He would remain overhead to keep the enemy away as long as his fuel held out, perhaps another 45min. [He] requested other flights to take over the top cover until a helicopter could be dispatched from Kimpo, 85mi [135 km] southwest, to come pick Bolt out. It was by then approximately 7:30 A.M. on a crisp, clear autumn morning *when the entire air war over Korea stopped* [Biteman's emphasis], just to cover Don Bolt.

"Every FEAF fighter airplane in the air was suddenly dedicated to the protection of Don Bolt, who was by then sitting dejectedly on the wing of his downed Mustang, watching the ever-changing flights of fighters circling overhead. Ground targets took second priority as MELLOW Control coordinated the air effort to keep a minimum of four fighters circling in the immediate area at all times, watching to assure that no troops attempted to close in on Bolt.

"Meanwhile, attempts were being made to line up a helicopter and crew. We did not know, until then, however, that *the maximum range of those ancient, early H-5 helicopters was less than 150mi [241 km]:* there was no way that they could fly from Kimpo to Pyongyang to pick up Bolt and have any chance of returning to friendly territory [Biteman's emphasis]. Still, the combat air patrol (CAP) remained overhead all through the day, dipping low periodically to strafe between the trees and Bolt's ship, to remind the Red troops to stay away.

"By mid-afternoon there were troops surrounding the entire field, and Don lay hunched low behind the wing. He had apparently been shot at while sitting on the wing. Each succeeding flight of circling fighters found it necessary to fire a burst of machine gun fire to keep the troops back behind the trees.

"Still, no means could be devised to pick Don out of his menacing circle. Finally, as dusk turned to darkness, after scores of combat sorties were diverted to protect him, Maj. Arnold 'Moon' Mullins flew our last patrol. Bolt was seen alive and still crouched beneath his Mustang. Moon said that he was sorely tempted to strafe the entire circle of enemy troops and vehicles but didn't dare: surely such action would be the single act to trigger the killing, on the spot, of Don Bolt.

"Mullins might as well have strafed the Red troops. A week later, after our forces took Pyongyang, the Graves Registration people found Bolt's body buried in a shallow grave just a short distance from his airplane. He had been shot in the back of the head, execution style."

My own Mustang bailout came on 5 October 1950 in aircraft 44-84982, that had 442hr on it and had previously belonged to the Nevada ANG. I was forced to bail out in North Korea only three days after we lost Bolt. My wingman aborted on takeoff, so I

Major Richard (Dick) Lewer of No. 2 Cheetah Squadron, SAAF, is seen in the cockpit of his F-51D Mustang at Korea's Hoengsong airfield on completion of his final combat mission on 21 September 1952. Lewer is the only South African pilot who fought in Korea and in his country's later border wars. Lewer's 6 July 1952 mishap was a memorable example of the difficult flying circumstances encountered by his countrymen who served as a part of the USAF's 18th FBW during the Korean fighting. *Richard Lewer*

proceeded with my element composed of Capt. Danny Leake and a new chap on his first mission, a first lieutenant named Mario DiSylvestro. We were assigned on an interdiction mission and instructed to attack targets of opportunity in an area north of Pyongyang.

While making a run on a camouflaged group of motor vehicles, I was struck by ground fire. There is an unmistakable "thunk" when you are hit, so I immediately pulled up and headed west toward the Yellow Sea to position myself for an SA-16 Air Rescue Albatross in case I went down.

Mustang Bailout

I was amazed to find that everything was still "in the green" on the instrument panel and the controls all worked properly. I asked Danny Leake to come in

An F-51D Mustang (no. 383) of No. 2 Cheetah Squadron, SAAF, operating in Korea in 1952. Maj. Richard (Dick) Lewer of No. 2 Squadron flew this particular aircraft on several combat sorties. *Richard Lewer*

and give me a good look over to see if there was any visible damage.

There wasn't. Then I made my first mistake of the day. I ordered us back to the target and we completed the mission. On the way home at 7,000ft, I was smoking a cigarette and writing up my mission report when Danny called and said, "Push your throttle up, Ed. You're falling back."

I didn't even look up—just pushed the throttle forward to what I figured was four or five inches of mercury and kept on writing.

Danny's second call was more urgent. "Push your throttle forward, Ed. Your air speed is falling off."

That brought my head up with a snap and, sure enough, the gauges were all unwinding. The old girl (the group commander's personal aircraft) had just quit flying!

For those who enjoy detective work, the question is, how many clues exist in this photo to tell us whether it was taken in 1944 or 1994? Hint: color film was readily available in drug stores in the United States in both years. Strongest clues, perhaps, are the non-standard pilot's seat back and the US civil registry number (NL3751D) visible slightly ahead of, and beneath, the horizontal stabilizer. Perhaps the only other clue is that *Hurry Home, Honey* is so beautifully pristine, lacking any smudges, oil smears, dents, or prangs. The date is 22 May 1994 and this is Charles Osborn's beautifully restored fighter in which the author received two orientation flights.

From any angle, it is a thing of beauty. The mixture of Army khaki and natural metal is based upon actual markings. Neither fighter pilot Brad Hood (front seat) nor would-be ace Dorr are wearing authentic clothing or equipment, but the aircraft itself is as authentic as it can be. One minor departure from the markings on the real Mustang that inspired this ship: on the real one, the "kill" markings were German crosses rather than swastikas. This angle is an especially good study of the bubble-canopy design that improved the Mustang's visibility.

This was of course a very serious development since I was still well inside North Korea and the lines thus far were still "liquid" and roughly in the neighborhood of the 38th Parallel. I was almost directly north of what was later to be called Panmunjom. I didn't know how far—it later turned out to be about 35mi north of the 38th Parallel. Knowing what had happened to Don Bolt, I determined to stretch my glide south as far as possible in hopes of reaching the range of the choppers at Kimpo. I immediately dropped my external tanks to reduce drag and set up the most efficient glide angle to "stretch" the glide. I fully intended to belly it in, so I tightened all my harness straps, popped the canopy, and prepared for a crash landing.

As I dragged the Mustang over a last ridge, I could see that the crash landing was a bad idea. Ahead was a small "bowl" with several rice paddies not nearly large enough for a successful crash landing. I dove down the side of the hill, pulled up till I could feel it stall, and leaped over the right side of the aircraft (which was the wrong side) at an altitude of 700ft, indicated. This was mountainous terrain so I knew I was too damn low.

When I went out of that F-51, I found myself staring the vertical stabilizer right between the eyes and thought, "Well, this is it."

But the slipstream rolled me over and, combined with the airplane snapping to the left, I was "spanked" off the right elevator—and hard enough to tear the dinghy off my backpack. When I saw the dinghy floating around overhead I thought, "Oh, shit, the elevator ripped off the chute." But I still had a rip cord, so I pulled it.

I normally use a seat pack but my chute was in for repack, so I'd borrowed Ross Cree's for that mission. Ross was so short that the harness was uncomfortably tight on me. I'd cursed it the whole mission—but it saved my life. First, it padded my collision with the tail and, second, back packs open slightly faster than seat packs.

114

Abrupt Landing

I hit the rice paddy on the back swing. I saw three people cowering with their hands protecting their heads as my head snapped down when the chute opened. Before I even got out of my harness, I had my .45 out and was looking for them. They were gone. I think the airplane fell on them. Danny and DiSylvestro said they didn't see anyone near me, so that would pretty well confirm it.

In a later letter to my wife, I told her I couldn't tell the bailout story nearly as well as Danny Leake because he had a ringside seat on my wing. He says he sure wishes he had a movie of that crash to sell to a film company. He said it scared him to death to see me ride it so low, come out, bounce off the tail, pop the chute, and hit the ground with my .45 out right beside the plane. I guess the whole incident only took 10sec.

Anyway, I got out of the chute and headed for higher ground, still worried about the three North Koreans I couldn't locate. As I ran up the side of the hill, explosions from the airplane and cooked-off ammo were going off all around me. About halfway up, I stumbled into an old slit trench and thought it would be a good place to hole up while I took stock of myself and the situation.

As I looked back down at the F-51 Mustang (now a smoking hole in the ground bearing no resemblance to an airplane at all and occasionally belching a cooked-off .50cal round), and spread-out chute, I could see a trail of equipment—helmet, mae west, scarf, gloves, etc. Well, I sure couldn't hide there because that trail led right to me!

I pulled out all my extra .45 clips—I think I had five or six spares stashed in my flying suit—and laid them out in front of me. I don't know why—I never could hit anything with that damn thing. Maybe I planned to scare them to death with the noise!

Mario [DiSylvestro] kept buzzing me to keep the North Koreans away and Danny [Leake] went upstairs and screamed for help. Thank God for a seasoned combat veteran to take up this rescue caper. Poor Mario was on his first mission. (Mario was later to make almost a career of covering bailed-out pilots, covering some five or six after me). I was pretty sure I'd gotten far enough south to be within chopper range of Kimpo. I knew it would be hopeless farther north. Either that morning [5 October] or the day

before, Daniel [Chappie] James and Damon B. [Stupe] Davis were on a mission way up near Sinanju when Stupe had to belly in on a sand bar. He jumped out and disappeared into trees and brush. Of course Chappie started screaming for help on "Guard" [the emergency channel], and I answered. When they told me where they were and what Davis had done, I advised him to leave the area and let our boy try some E&E [escape and evasion]. I don't know if Stupe ever got out.

In about an hour, two Marine F4U Corsairs showed up and relieved Danny and Mario. In about another hour, here come two more Corsairs weaving around over top of this chopper—I think it was the first one I'd ever seen and the most beautiful sight in the world. I ran back down the hill, picked up my hard hat and the rip cord (yes, I still have it) and stood on my chute.

The helicopter landed right beside me, took me aboard, and we got the hell out of there. Danny and Mario were waiting for me on the ramp at Kimpo. I can't describe the feeling of elation as we rushed to hug each other.

Later in the war, Danny Leake was killed in action when he was also forced to bail out and struck the tail. I hope to God he wasn't trying to emulate me, because I did everything wrong and got away with it. You're supposed to go out the left side and dive for the wing root. This will allow you to go under the elevator because of the slipstream (so they say). I knew I didn't have enough altitude to follow the script and just *leaped*!

Maj. Richard (Dick) Lewer, No. 2 Cheetah Squadron, SAAF

It was 6 July 1952. I was serving as a 22-year-old fighter-bomber pilot flying Mustang F-51Ds with the SAAF No. 2 Cheetah Squadron, part of the USAF's 18th FBW, in Korea. I had completed 17 sorties over North Korea. These were rail and road interdiction missions along the mountainous and rugged front line that stretched from the east to the west coast.

At this stage of the Korean War, the Second World War-vintage Mustangs were getting a bit capped and had already cost the lives of several of our pilots in crashes due to mechanical failure. Apart from this minor failing, it was a beautiful aircraft to fly, with virtually no limits apart from over G-ing the pilot after pulling out from vertical bombing dives. Our expert ground crews maintained the aircraft in the best possible condition.

On the day in question I was one of a four-plane flight that had already made radio and visual contact with the airborne forward air controller during a close-support mission. In this mountainous and rugged section of the front line, it was virtually impossible to differentiate between our own and the enemy positions. These positions were often only a few hundred meters apart and comprised well dug-in

This P-51D Mustang (44-14868) was the second ship to be nicknamed *Hurry Home, Honey*. This plane was flown by Capt. Richard A. "Pete" Peterson, an ace of the 364th FS/357th FG credited with 15.5 aerial victories. The flight view of 44-14868 was taken by Cpl. E. W. "Bill" Peveroff, gunner of a flak-crippled B-17G Flying Fortress (43-38385) nicknamed *Sugah* that probably would not have made it home but for the efforts of Mustang pilot Peterson. By this juncture, Peterson had already racked up most of his 15.5 aerial victories. *USAF via Merle C. Olmsted*

These pilots of the 364th FS/357th FG were the real-life inspiration for the love of World War II fighters that motivates today's warbird movement. Left to right, they are 1st Lt. Hollis (Bud) Nowin, 1st Lt. Mark Stepelton, Capt. Richard A. "Pete" Peterson, and 1st Lt. Louis Fecher. Air ace Peterson inspired today's warbird *Hurry Home, Honey* painted to represent the first P-51D Mustang in which he scored many of his air-to-air victories in Europe. Nearly half a century after the fight over Europe, Peterson had flown in the warbird shortly before this volume went to press. *USAF via Merle C. Olmsted*

and camouflaged bunkers, gun and mortar positions, and trenches. To positively identify the target, the forward air controller would fire a smoke rocket called a "Woolie Peter" [usually called "Willie Peter" by Americans and meaning white phosphorus] in the direction of the position to be attacked and would then direct the fighters onto the target by giving close directions and distance from his rocket burst. During attacks every enemy soldier opened fire on the diving aircraft with their automatic weapons, and the tracers and air bursts made a spectacular display.

On this occasion, the target was a battery of well dug-in and camouflaged gun positions several miles behind enemy lines, and the controller had already fired his smoke rocket and directed us onto the target. Low cloud covered the area, and as we were equipped with two 500lb [227kg] bombs per aircraft, it was necessary to commence the dive from minimum safe altitude.

I had just rolled in for my attack when thick smoke suddenly started pouring out of the engine and oil streamed over the canopy. After checking that my sight was more or less on the target, I released the bombs and eased out of the dive with a sick feeling in my stomach. Unfortunately, most pilots assume bad luck only happens to others. This was wishful thinking.

My first instinct was to head for our lines at full throttle. I may mention that we had been briefed that North Korean troops occupied this portion of the front line. The Chinese troops were regarded as bad news, but the North Koreans were right at the bottom of the popularity list. Horrific stories of what they did to captured pilots were common.

Fortunately, common sense prevailed, and I reduced power to nurse the engine and carried out a careful check of the engine instruments. The oil pressure was falling, and it did not take much imagination to realize that an oil pipe had ruptured. Smoke and oil were still pouring out from the engine and the forward visibility through the front of the bulletproof glass was virtually nil.

At this stage, I was approximately 1,000ft (309m) above the crests of the very rugged mountains, and the other three Mustangs were flying in comforting proximity to me.

Suddenly I spotted a small dirt airstrip in a valley and realized that I had crossed out of enemy territory. Small airstrips were scattered immediately behind the front line to evacuate badly wounded soldiers. These strips were designed for single-engine Cessna and Stinson L-5 aircraft. In the circumstances, I had no choice but to try and land as soon as possible on the strip that I had spotted.

The approach was nerve wracking as I realized that the engine would seize immediately when the oil pressure dropped to near zero and my altitude was too low to attempt to bail out if this occurred. Apart from the airstrip the boulder-strewn ground below was most unsuitable even for a wheels-up landing.

The forward visibility, due to the thick layer of oil on the windscreen, did not improve matters. I carried out a curved approach, aiming to hit the runway at its very beginning and at minimum airspeed.

With a combination of good luck and good judgment, and using maximum brakes, I managed to achieve my aim and stopped in a cloud of dust at the end of the short runway. The aircraft was undamaged, apart from the fractured oil pipe. I had switched the engine off on touchdown and as I clambered out

The wartime *Hurry Home, Honey* (44-13586, coded C5-T) became the inspiration for the beautifully restored warbird, which flies 50 years later looking almost exactly like the original. The aircraft had khaki upper surfaces, tail, and wings but is otherwise natural metal. *USAF via Merle C. Olmsted*

of the cockpit of the now completely oil-smeared Mustang, I was surrounded by a group of American medical orderlies who lived in a tent next to the airstrip. Beers were pressed into my hands, and I was feted like a being from outer space. The orderlies never believed they would see a fighter landing on their strip and were thrilled with all the excitement. As far as I am aware, I was the only Mustang pilot that landed on one of the emergency front-line strips without damaging the aircraft.

After my landing, the rest of the flight flew low overhead in greeting and returned to base. Later that same day I had my first flight in a helicopter that took me back to our forward base at K-46 and I was back flying operational sorties the next day. I was pushing hard to fly as many operational sorties as possible on every trip to our forward base at K-46 as I wanted to complete my tour of 75 sorties in time to return home for the start of the university year (I had interrupted my studies to volunteer for service in Korea). In the circumstances I later regretted that I had not taken

four days off from operations to return to the downed Mustang with the ground crew who repaired the engine, stripped the aircraft down to minimum weight, and used my old friend Capt. (later Colonel) Attie Bosch to fly it safely back to base.

A footnote: of the seven replacement pilots who went to Korea with me, only three of us completed our tours. On 23 July 1951 Capt. F. M. Bekker led a section of Mustangs of No. 2 Squadron to destroy a bridge over the Imjin River, Korea, despite poor visibility. Low clouds forced them to fly below 200m. Heavy AA fire shot down Captain Bekker in Mustang 335 as well as two other F-51Ds. It was the heaviest single mission loss suffered by No. 2 Squadron during the Korean War.

Robert F. Dorr, author

A stubborn wet chill hangs in the glassy air. It's 6:45 A.M. Just after dawn. Sunday, May 22, 1994. No one has arrived. The airfield is empty, expectant. Dew shimmers on rivets, canopies, and wing leading edges. It's air-show day.

Soon, maybe as soon as 7:00 or 7:30 a.m, a trickle of local North Carolina folk will arrive to prepare today's aerial gala, the annual "Warbirds over Hickory" fly-in. And by the time the gates open at ten, people will be everywhere. Pilots, crew chiefs, security, vendors, medics, wing walkers. They'll be all over the Hickory Regional Airport while engines cough, smoke wafts along with the garlic and hot-dog smells, and the crowds pour in.

In the throng soon to come will be ten thousand who'd like to fly in a P-51 Mustang. Dozens will have a strong claim. One air-show ticket holder flew Mustangs with the 4th FG over Berlin 50 years ago. Another devoted thousands of hours to historical preservation. Many have traveled miles to *touch* a Mustang, and would give an arm and a leg to *fly* in a Mustang. They won't, today. And they might deem fate unkind if they knew this author was getting the opportunity *twice*.

But at 6:45 A.M. not a single human being can be seen at the airport except pilot Brad Hood squirting Windex on the canopy of the Mustang he flies.

Plus the author, pulling on a Styrofoam cup of convenience-store coffee.

"Want to go up again?" Brad asks.

"Are you *serious*?" The previous day, Brad and I spent an hour aloft in the P-51D. It had been a privilege.

"I came here to fly, Bob."

So while they trickle in—a handful, then dozens, of men and women who'll make this air show happen, Brad Hood and I wriggle into chutes. You plant your right foot in the "step" behind the left wing trailing edge, swing your left leg up on the wing root, climb in, and strap in.

The aircraft is Charles Osborn's pristine P-51D-25-NA Mustang (44-73206) registered as NL3751D. It's painted with wartime invasion stripes as *Hurry Home, Honey* (44-13586, coded C5-T) as flown by Capt. Richard A. "Pete" Peterson, an ace of the 357th FG credited with 15.5 aerial victories.

Beautiful job

The plane has been restored to its realistic configuration with exquisite care. From the tip of the propeller hub to the rear of the rudder trailing edge, it's difficult to find anything that couldn't be a component on an authentic, 1944 Mustang. Perhaps the only unrealistic feature of *Hurry Home, Honey* is its cleanliness, for this artifact of our heritage is treated as a treasure, while wartime Mustangs rarely had time for a bath. Then there's Brad's modern-day helmet and our Cessna T-37-style parachutes—otherwise, nothing to reveal that it's now a half-century later and we aren't cranking up to escort Flying Fortresses to Berlin.

In a Mustang, the start-up is impressive. Brad's Merlin kicks in smoothly and doesn't seem very loud. The Mustang chafes at the bit, like any tail-dragger straining against its brakes. Fumes engulf the cockpit. "They get into your eyes, your face, your hair," Brad acknowledges. The first vivid smell of a combat mission was those fumes, pouring into the open canopy and staying there, filling tie air, clawing at the eyes, nostrils, mouth.

With help from wing-walkers and hand-wavers, Brad Hood turns the P-51D Mustang on its generous wheelbase and begins trundling smoothly toward runway's end at Hickory, North Carolina, talking to the tower on a radio more modern than any used in the European war. The rear seat is comfortable but small and close-up against Brad's, so that this backseater has almost the same view as the guy flying the plane. Brad is also on the headset.

"We're clear to take off," he tells me. It's deceptive. He's busy on the radio and is poring over a checklist, yet the illusion persists that he's doing this by instinct. Brad slides the canopy shut. No more fumes. He checks coolant and oil temperatures, sets the mixture to run, puts the stick back, and begins a run-up to around 2,300rpm.

He accelerates into the turn, beginning the take-off roll the instant he's centered on the yellow line.

Taking off in a Mustang, depending upon the aircraft weight, you apply 10deg of flaps—or none. The book says to advance the throttle to maximum while brakes are still on, then release the brakes. Veterans recall it being rare to drop flaps when the runway was long enough: combat pilots preferred to conserve the engine and "fly it off" with the least power essential to the task. Where there's sufficient runway, you don't need "max" power, just "climb" power. To improve visibility quickly, you can raise the tail early—putting forward pressure on the stick to bring down the elevator lifts the tail—but as we'll see, most pilots don't.

On our flight in *Hurry Home, Honey*, I'm too enraptured by the ambiance to notice whether Brad chooses flaps or goes to full throttle. The beginning of the roll, the rotation, the pull-off, all proceed with a seamless grace.

Liftoff in the Mustang occurs between 100 and 105mph (160 and 168km/h). Pilots accustomed to lightweight tail-draggers like that idea of lifting the Mustang's rear end quickly, but most recommend keeping tail wheel on pavement as long as possible for positive control. Seconds tick away before Brad pulls our tail wheel off.

He lifts the nose. In a smooth, swift transition, *Hurry Home, Honey* pokes its nose at the few clouds dangling high above us. Once airborne, you pull on the handle to raise the gear and take the throttle back to climb power. One World War II veteran remembers the Mustang for its "nice comfortable cockpit" but "better human engineering" in the roomier P-47 Thunderbolt.

Seen at Hickory, North Carolina, (site of one of the nation's finest warbird shows) on 22 May 1994 is Charles Osborn's beautifully restored P-51D-25-NA Mustang (44-73206) registered as NL3751D. *USAF via Merle C. Olmsted*

Climbing Away

Brad uses stick and rudder for a sharp, steep bank over the airfield. This provides a spectacular glance at the parking area beginning to fill, the lines forming at the gate, the other early stirrings of one of the great warbird air shows becoming more and more popular all over the US.

Above and facing page
It's impossible to avoid illustrating three more eye-pleasing World War II fighters, a Mustang and two Mustang contemporaries, which appeared at the 22 May 1994 warbirds event in Hickory, North Carolina. NAA P-51D N51YS **[Left top]** belongs to Steve Collins. Republic P-47D-25-RA Thunderbolt 44-90368, registered as N4747P, belongs to Charles Osborn **[Left bottom]** and is painted to represent 44-32773, coded S-4P, nicknamed *Big Ass Bird II*, flown by Lt. Howard Park of the 406th FG in Europe. Vought F4U-5NL Corsair (bureau number 124560, registered as NX9401W) belongs to Dave Burnap **[Above]**. None of these aircraft or owners will resolve the long-standing dispute over which was the best fighter of World War II, but most would agree that the P-51 Mustang is more than a leading candidate. *Jim Sullivan*

From beneath, our flying filly is a real eye-stopper. Later, the 4th FG veteran, walking through the airfield gate as we hurl skyward, will tell me how it touched his heartstrings, seeing this sleek fighter depart the airfield pattern and head for the heavens.

Contrary to myth, the Mustang is not a fast climber. Although no wartime fighter in its class is faster in level flight (or has longer range), the Mustang's climb rate is 14 percent less than that of the Spitfire Mark IX, 17 percent less than that of the Messerschmitt Bf 109G. In the back seat of our aircraft, almost rubbing my nose against Brad's helmet, it's hard to tell. *Hurry Home, Honey* feels like a homesick angel.

Brad flies the Mustang out over the lakes and waterways near Hickory, where some palatial homes abut the water and a few boats are chugging around. The sky is perfect. No wind, no turbulence, nothing. "Want to see a few maneuvers?" he asks.

"No. I wouldn't want anything like that."

Brad understands that this means "Yes." He demonstrates an aileron roll. You go into this 360deg

roll by building up a little G—the equivalent of gravity forces, of which the decrepit author can handle only about three or four—then slipping the plane into the wing-over. Again, the progression is smooth.

Flight Handling

Is the smoothness deceptive? No aircraft has a more pleasing aerodynamic shape. In most flight regimes, pilots call the Mustang a somewhat heavy, very stable platform. But they also urge a thorough knowledge of the aircraft coupled with alertness and caution. Outside its intended flight envelope, the Mustang can become a "widow maker."

Most pilots believe that stability and control authority were sacrificed with the change from the Allison to the Merlin engine. To varying degrees, the engine change reduced stability in all three axes. A

Above and facing page
More views of today's *Hurry Home, Honey* a beautifully restored P-51D Mustang.

narrow chord, three-blade propeller gave way to a heavier, broad chord, four-blade version. The fuselage was deepened, and addition of a fuselage fuel tank produced the potential for serious center-of-gravity problems. There is only one cure for this. The pilot must know his stuff. He also must be aware and alert, always.

With the greenery of North Carolina sweeping past beneath *Hurry Home, Honey,* Brad conducts a series of turns with increasing angles of bank as our flight unfolds. The need to lead with rudder to aid a maneuver becomes evident, and this improves the initial roll rate. After some rehearsal, we're doing climbing turns at 130mph (208km/h). All the time the pilot retains good control authority. As a natural next step, Brad takes us into practicing stalls.

Remarkably, there are some warbird fliers who have never intentionally stalled their Mustangs, never flown them upside down, and never practiced emergency procedures for an engine failure after takeoff. Some of these pilots (a category that decidedly does not include Osborn and Hood) ought to be grounded. With more money than sense, they fly in bad weather without an IFR (instrument flight rules) rating and embark on long voyages without adequate cross-country experience. One pilot underwent a "few hours" of ground school, sat in the back seat for two hops, and then proclaimed himself ready to tackle almost any aerial task in the Mustang. Fortunately, most who fly restored fighters are a more serious and more sensible breed.

Brad Hood wrings out the P-51D over forests, lakes, and waterfront homes near Hickory. He does gentle mock strafing, then turns and rolls. They call it the Cadillac of the Skies. The Mustang seems to perform exactly as the pilot asks. No complaints. No squawks.

"Okay, we're going to strafe that dam below us."

Hurry Home, Honey goes into a dive. You try to imagine what it must have been like—the real thing. You're rushing downward. On a real mission, the pilot would have his thumb on the trigger. The sewing-machine buzz of the six .50cal guns would be audible. You'd see geysers flying up from the water—not one after another like in the movies, but all at the same instant as hundreds of rounds of ammunition hit home simultaneously. If this were the real thing, you'd have to worry about the vulnerability of that radiator under your seat, about the need to pull out at exactly the right instant . . .

Heading back toward Hickory airfield, I can see Brad busy getting ready for our landing. Looking for other traffic, we see—and are told—that we own the sky all the way down to the ground. Brad switches gas to the main tank and fuel boost to on. As speed drops below 170mph (272 km/h), he lowers the gear and checks the green lights as we bank into the pattern for a short approach. Brad sets the prop to 2,700rpm. He checks temperatures and pressures. Over his shoulder, this back-seater catches a view of the airfield—now filling to capacity with an air-show crowd.

Author Robert F. Dorr (back seat) struggles to peer over pilot Brad Hood's shoulder as today's *Hurry Home, Honey* is preflighted for a mission into the wild blue yonder. *Jim Sullivan*

If you had one of these, wouldn't you keep it clean? In a revealing close-up, modern-day Mustang pilot Brad Hood is observed spray-cleaning the inside of *Hurry Home, Honey*'s bubble canopy.

Brad lowers flaps to 10deg. We turn a short final and now there's more flap applied. The landing is smooth and easy. We taxi in, aided now by wing walkers, and turn the P-51D Mustang into its parking place. Friends and strangers are gathering around the aircraft when this back-seater finally clambers out. My flights in *Hurry Home, Honey*—two of them—may not have proven much that was new or profound about the P-51D Mustang, but they are the perfect icing on the cake after months of writing about the aircraft. The Mustang is exactly what our 4th group veteran calls it—"a super ship to fly."

P-51 Mustang Serial Numbers

NAA P-51s

Designation	S/N	Quantity
NA-73X	NX19998	1
Subtotal		1
Mustang I	AG345/AG664	320
Mustang I	AL958/AL999	42
Mustang I	AM100/AM257	158
Mustang I	AP164/AP263	100
Subtotal		620
(XP-51)	41-038 (AG348)	(1)
	41-039 (AG354)	(1)
Subtotal		(2)
P-51-NA	41-37320/37351	32
	41-37353/37420	68
	41-37422/37469	48
Subtotal		128
P-51A-NA*	43-6003/6312	310
Subtotal		310
XP-51B	41-37352	1
	41-37421	1
Subtotal		2
P-51B-NA*	42-106429/106538	110
	42-106541/106978	438
	43-6313/7202	890
	43-12093/12492	400
	43-24752/24901	150
Subtotal		1,990
P-51C-NT*	42-102979/103978	1,000
	43-24902/25251	350
	44-10753/11152	400
Subtotal		1,750
P-51D-NA	42-106539/106540	2
	44-12853/15752	2,900
	44-72027/75026	3,000
	44-84390/84989	600
P-51D-NT*	44-11153/11352	200
	44-63160/64159	1,000
	45-11343/11742	400
Subtotal		8,102
XP-51F-NA	43-43332/43334	3
Subtotal		3
XP-51G-NA	43-43335/43336	2
Subtotal		2
P-51H-NA	44-64160/64714	555
Subtotal		555
XP-51J-NA	44-76027/76028	2
Subtotal		2
P-51K-NT*	44-11353/12852	1,500
Subtotal		1,500
P-51M-NT	45-11743	1
Subtotal		1
A-36A-NA	42-83663/84162	500
Subtotal		500

Total of NAA-built P-51s:
15,463

CAVALIER MUSTANGS

Designation	S/N	Quantity
F-51D (Cavalier)	67-14862/14865	4
	67-22579/22582	4
	68-15795/15796	2
	72-1536/1541	6
TF-51D (Cavalier)	67-14866	1
Turbo Mustang	N201PE, N202PE	2
Subtotal		19

Total of Cavalier-built F-51s: 19

PIPER ENFORCER

Piper PA-48 Enforcer	N481PE/N482PE	2
Subtotal		2
Total of Piper Enforcers		2

COMMONWEALTH MUSTANGS

Designation	Mark (S/N)	Quantity
CA-17	20 (A68-1/80)	80
CA-18	22 (A68-81/94)	14
CA-18	21 (A68-95/120)	26
CA-18	23 (68-121/186)	66
CA-18	22 (A68-187/200)	14
Total of Commonwealth-built aircraft:		200
Total of Mustangs built:		**15,684**

*P-51A-NA total includes 35 F-6B; P-51B-NA total includes 71 F-6C; P-51C total includes 20 F-6C; P-51D-NT total includes 146 F-6D; P-51K-NT total includes 163 F-6K, resulting in a total of 435 F-6s (35 F-6B, 91 F-6C, 146 F-6D, 163 F-6K)

Bibliography

Coggan, Paul A. *Mustang Survivors*. Bourne End, Bucks: Aston Publications, 1987.

Cull, Brian, and Shlomo Aloni, with David Nicolle. *Spitfires Over Israel: The First Authoritative Account of the Air Conflict During the Israeli War of Independence, 1948–49*. London: Grub Street, 1992.

Davis, Larry. *P-51 Mustang in Action*. Carrollton, Texas: Squadron Signal, 1981.

Dienst, John, and Dan Hagedorn. *North American F-51 Mustangs in Latin American Air Force Service*. Arlington, Texas: Aerofax, 1985.

Dorr, Robert F., and David Donald. *Fighters of the United States Air Force*. London: Aerospace, 1990

Ethell, Jeffrey. *Mustang: A Documentary History*. London: Jane's, 1981.

Freeman, Roger A. *Combat Profile Mustang: The P-51 Merlin Mustang in World War 2*. Shepperton: Ian Allan, 1989.

Green, William and John Fricker. *The Air Forces of the World*. London: Hanover House, 1958.

Hall, Ake (ed.) *J(S)26 Mustang*. Kontaktgruppen for Flyghistorisk Forskning (Swedish Aviation Historical Research Group), Hisings Backa, Sweden, 1980.

Jackson, Robert. *P-51 Mustang: The Operational Record*. London: Airlife, 1992.

Olmsted, Merle C. *The Yoxford Boys: The 357th FG on Escort over Europe and Russia*. Fallbrook, California: Aero Publishers, 1971.

Wilson, Stewart. *The Spitfire, Mustang and Kittyhawk in Australian Service*. Weston Creek, Australia: Aerospace Publications, 1988.

Index